GORGIAS

D0109678

The Library of Liberal Arts
OSKAR PIEST, FOUNDER

GORGIAS

PLATO

Translated, with an introduction, by
W. C. HELMBOLD

The Library of Liberal Arts
published by
Bobbs-Merrill Educational Publishing
INDIANAPOLIS

The Bobbs-Merrill Company, Inc.
4300 West 62nd Street
Indianapolis, Indiana 46268

First Edition
Twenty-fifth Printing — 1985

Library of Congress Catalog Card Number: 52–9226
ISBN 0–672–60181–8 (pbk)

CONTENTS

INTRODUCTION

Gorgias' profession, the teaching of rhetoric, and the right and wrong uses of rhetoric itself are, at least technically, the themes of this work; and it is in reference to these that the dialogue is developed until it finally transcends them. Gorgias himself is handled as gently as circumstances permit; Polus, his acknowledged pupil, and Callicles, his host and perhaps his spiritual disciple, bear the brunt of the drubbing administered to the 'science' of rhetoric as it was practiced in Plato's youth. (It is probable that Gorgias came to Athens in the very year of Plato's birth.)

The *Gorgias,* like the rest of Plato, may be viewed on several levels. For the general reader, or in the initial reading, one of the more fruitful approaches is to regard the work as a study in what may happen when an attentive mind asks a simple question and pursues the answers to their natural conclusions. In this case the apparently guileless query, "What is Gorgias' profession?" leads, in the end, to an examination of how life itself should be lived and how rhetoric is to be linked to the Good Life. The aim of true rhetoric, we may be sure, is nothing other than improvement and education; the only proper use of persuasion is to make us better. But are we, then, incapable of making a true use of rhetoric ourselves until we have been improved by its offices? What happens in the meantime, until the desired conversion has been effected? Here, Plato might say, is the place for Socrates. This is the value of great and wise men: we must listen to them, the mouthpieces of true rhetoric, until we are in a position to think and speak for ourselves. Once we have become capable of wise and prudent action, we may enter politics or whatever profession of wisdom we choose. That is the final point of Socrates' concluding speech.

To Plato the Good Life is something more intense than we creatures of a paler emotional climate are able to achieve, or even comprehend. Some critics prefer the *Gorgias* to other more complex dialogues because there is here no irrationality, no hint of divine madness. But even here the passion for truth reaches an emotional intensity which must invigorate everyone capable of sharing it. It may be, as Housman lightly remarks, that the passion for truth is the faintest of human emotions—in the rest of us; but in Plato it burned at such heat that we may still be warmed by its incandescence. Accordingly we may note in the second half of the dialogue, the Callicles section, that the emotional tone is heightened and a real urgency imparted to a seemingly remote and academic question by ominous foreshadowings of Socrates' own death at the hands of bad rhetoric and worse politics. It is part of the irony that an unjust death did come to Socrates; and it *may* be part of the emotional implication that Callicles (who is otherwise unknown) may have had some share, if only an indirect one, in the sinister trial of 399. This, however, is mere conjecture, suggested by the fact that he remains unconvinced throughout the argument. So far as Plato allows us to know, Callicles may have merely laughed or sighed or shaken hands all around when Socrates' final speech reached its great conclusion. This is a standard pattern of behavior: we are embarrassed by great passions; worse, we are confounded when they are raised to the highest intellectual and moral plane.

The *Gorgias* may serve as a propaedeutic for the *Phaedrus*, one of the chief aims of which is to give an account of what rhetoric should be. Later, Aristotle, in his masterly treatment of the subject, was at considerable pains to obviate Plato's chief criticisms; i.e., that rhetoric is only a knack like cookery and that it is immoral, since it is used wholesale for the furtherance of the worst possible ends. Aristotle was able to answer such charges with considerable success; and, in fact, Plato had already shown the way to the right use of rhetoric (and dialectic) in his dialogues, among which the present work is one of the most brilliant and most successful.

Nothing need be added here concerning the differences between dialectic and rhetoric except to note the practical difference suggested by the contrasts between the examination of Polus (dialectic), the great speech of Callicles (wrong rhetoric in its most vigorous and dangerous form), and the final speech of Socrates (true rhetoric). If the reader will pay careful attention to the instructions and criticisms which Socrates gives to his successive interlocutors, he will receive, in addition to much enjoyment, an excellent schooling in the technique of argumentation and even in the etiquette, so to speak, of dialectic.

The translator has consulted other English versions and wishes to acknowledge his debt especially to Cope for valuable suggestions he received from that excellent source. For numerous improvements a considerable obligation is also due to Mr. Irwin Titunik, to Professors Benson Mates and W. B. Holther of the University of California, and to Dr. Martin Ostwald of Columbia University who have criticized portions of the MS, and to Mr. Robert Keenlyside who has read it all. The translator is further greatly obliged to the patient work of The Liberal Arts Press and to its editor, Mr. Oskar Piest, for a great many improvements in style and disposition.

Burnet's Oxford text, with minor changes, has been followed throughout. In a few cases the translator has ventured to bracket passages which appear to be interpolations, ancient editors' additions or explanations which do not seem to have proceeded from Plato himself.

W. C. HELMBOLD

THE UNIVERSITY OF CALIFORNIA
December, 1951

SELECTED BIBLIOGRAPHY

Burnet, J., *Greek Philosophy, Part I, Thales to Plato*. London, 1924.

Friedländer, Paul, *Platon*. 2 v. Berlin, 1928-30.

Gomperz, Th., *Greek Thinkers*. New York, 1905.

Grote, G., *Plato and Other Companions of Socrates*. London, 1867.

Linforth, Ivan Mortimore, *Soul and Sieve in Plato's Gorgias*. "University of California Publications in Classical Philology," v. XII, pp. 295-315. Berkeley, 1944.

Pater, W., *Plato and Platonism*. London, 1925.

Pohlenz, Max, *Aus Platos Werdezeit: Philologische Untersuchungen*, Berlin, 1913.

Räder, Hans, *Platons philosophische Entwickelung*. Leipzig, 1905.

Ritter, Constantin, *The Essence of Plato's Philosophy*. Tr. by Adam Alles. London, 1933.

Shorey, Paul, *What Plato Said*. Chicago, 1933.

Wilamowitz-Moellendorff, Ulrich von, *Platon, sein Leben und seine Werke*. 3rd ed. Berlin, 1948.

GORGIAS

GORGIAS

Characters of the Dialogue

CALLICLES   SOCRATES   CHAEREPHON
GORGIAS   POLUS

SCENE: *The scene is at first a street in Athens, but soon
changes to the interior of Callicles' home*

Callicles. When there's any fighting going on, as they say, Socrates, this is the right time to arrive for it.

Socrates. So, as the same proverb says,[1] we've come too late for the feast?

Call. Yes, and it was an elegant repast, too. Only a little while ago Gorgias treated us to a fine long declamation.

Socr. Well really, the responsibility for that lies with Chaerephon here, for he kept us loitering in the market-place.

Chaerephon. Don't worry, Socrates, I'll find the remedy, too. Gorgias is a friend of mine and he'll declaim for us right now, if you like, or, if you'd rather, sometime later.

Call. What's this, Chaerephon? Does Socrates really want to listen to Gorgias?

Chaer. Of course. That's just what we've come for, you know.

Call. Well, if that's the case, why don't you come to my house whenever you like? Gorgias is staying with me and will be delighted to declaim for you.

Socr. A good idea, Callicles. But do you suppose he would be willing just to talk with us? What I really want is to learn from him the power of his art, and what it is that he professes to teach.

[1] Cf. also Shakespeare: "Well," says Falstaff,
"To the latter end of a fray and the beginning of a feast
Fits a dull fighter and a keen guest" (*Henry IV*. Pt. I, iv 2).

3

The rest of his performance he may, as you suggest, deliver at some other time.

Call. There's nothing like asking him, Socrates. His skill in conversation was, in fact, one of the points in his performance. Why, just now he urged all the company to ask whatever questions they wished and he promised to answer them all.

Socr. Splendid! [2] Chaerephon, question him!

Chaer. What shall I ask?

Socr. Who he is.

Chaer. How do you mean?

Socr. If, for example, he happened to be a maker of shoes, I suppose he would answer that he was a cobbler. Do you understand what I mean?

Chaer. I do. Tell me, Gorgias, is it true, as Callicles here claims, that you profess to answer whatever anyone asks you?

Gorgias. Quite true, Chaerephon. Just a short time ago, in fact, I made this very claim. I may add that it has been a good many years since I have been asked anything new.

Chaer. So I expect you find answering easy, Gorgias?

Gorg. Why don't you try and see, Chaerephon?

Polus. Well, for heaven's sake! Put your questions to me, Chaerephon, if you please. Gorgias, I'm afraid, is all tired out; as you know, he's been through a great deal of speaking already.

Chaer. Really, Polus? Do you think that you can make better answers than Gorgias?

Pol. What does that matter if they're good enough for you?

Chaer. No matter at all. Since you wish it, get ready to answer.

Pol. Ask away.

Chaer. I shall. If Gorgias were a master of the same art as his brother Herodicus, what name would it be proper to give him? The same as his brother?

Pol. Of course.

Chaer. Then we should be right in saying that he was a physician?

Pol. Yes.

---

[2] At this point the speakers arrive at Callicles' house. They find there Gorgias and his disciple, Polus, together with numerous auditors.

Chaer. And if he were conversant with the art of Aristophon, son of Aglaophon, or his brother,[3] by what name would it be proper to call him?

Pol. Obviously a painter.

Chaer. But as it is, of what art is he master and what name is the right name by which to call him?

Pol. Chaerephon, among mortals many arts have been discovered empirically from experience. For it is experience which makes our life proceed by art, but lack of experience which reduces it to chance. Various are the arts of which various men variously partake; but the best partake of the best. Gorgias here is of this company and so has a share in the noblest of the arts.

Socr. Really, Gorgias, Polus seems to be well prepared to make speeches. He is not, however, fulfilling his promise to Chaerephon.

Gorg. In what particular, Socrates?

Socr. He doesn't appear to be answering the question at all.

Gorg. Well then, if you like, ask him yourself.

Socr. No. But if you really don't mind answering questions yourself, I'd much rather ask you. For, to judge Polus by his own words, he seems to have had more practice in what is called rhetoric than in the give and take of discussion.

Pol. What do you mean, Socrates?

Socr. Merely, Polus, that when Chaerephon asked of what art Gorgias was a master, you delivered a eulogy of his art as though someone were blaming it; but you didn't answer what it was.

Pol. But I did! I said it was the noblest of all.

Socr. Quite so. But no one is asking what the art of Gorgias is like, but what it is, and what he should be called. Just as Chaerephon traced out for you the previous argument and you gave him good short answers, so now in the same way tell us what Gorgias' art is and what we ought to call him. Or better, tell us yourself, Gorgias, of what art you are master and by what name we should call you.

Gorg. Rhetoric, Socrates.

Socr. Then we should call you a rhetorician?

449

[3] The famous painter Polygnotus.

Gorg. And a good one, too, Socrates, if you wish to call me what 'I boast myself to be,' as Homer says.[4]

Socr. I shall be delighted to do so.

Gorg. Well then, do it.

Socr. Are we then to say that you are capable of making others rhetoricians?

Gorg. That is just what I do profess, not only here in Athens. but elsewhere as well.

Socr. Then would you be so kind, Gorgias, as to continue in the manner of our present conversation, asking and answering questions, and lay aside for a subsequent occasion the sort of lengthy exposition which Polus began? Don't deceive my hopes; keep your promise and be good enough to answer briefly what I ask you.

Gorg. There are some answers, Socrates, which must necessarily be stated at length; but I shall certainly try to give them as briefly as possible. This is, in fact, another of my professions: no one can say the same thing more succinctly than I.

Socr. That's just exactly what we want, Gorgias: give me a good specimen of your clipped style and we can reserve the full-dress for a later occasion.

Gorg. I shall be glad to do so. You'll say you've never heard anyone speak more briefly.

Socr. Very well. You say that you are master of the rhetorical art and can make anyone else a rhetorician. With what class of objects is rhetoric concerned? As, for example, the art of weaving is concerned with the manufacture of clothes, isn't it?

Gorg. Yes.

Socr. And likewise the musical art with the composition of songs?

Gorg. Yes.

Socr. Heavens, Gorgias! I'm certainly delighted with your replies; you answer in the very fewest possible words.

Gorg. Yes, Socrates, I believe I am doing rather nicely.

Socr. You certainly are. So give me the same sort of answer about rhetoric: with what class of objects does it deal as a science?

[4] *Il.* VI. 211 and often.

Gorg. With words.

Socr. What sort of words, Gorgias? Do you mean those that indicate to the sick what sort of treatment will make them well?

Gorg. No.

Socr. Then rhetoric is not concerned with all words?

Gorg. Of course not.

Socr. Yet it does make men able to speak?

Gorg. Yes.

Socr. And also to comprehend what they are talking about?

Gorg. Certainly.

Socr. But doesn't the art of medicine, which we just men- 450 tioned, make men capable of comprehending and speaking about the sick?

Gorg. It must.

Socr. Then medicine, too, it seems, is concerned with words.

Gorg. Yes.

Socr. Those, perhaps, concerned with diseases?

Gorg. Precisely.

Socr. Is the art of physical culture also concerned with words which relate to the good and the bad conditioning of bodies?

Gorg. To be sure.

Socr. And, moreover, Gorgias, the case is the same with all the other arts. Each of them is concerned with words, specific words which deal with the subject of each art.

Gorg. It looks that way.

Socr. Then why don't you call the other arts concerned with words rhetorical, if you give this name to an art which is concerned with words?

Gorg. Because, Socrates, in the other arts all the knowledge, so to speak, is concerned with manual labor and activities of that kind; but in rhetoric there is no such manual operation. All its activity and effectiveness is through words. For this reason I claim that the art of rhetoric is concerned with words, and I maintain that I am right in doing so.

Socr. Now I wonder whether I quite understand what sort of art you are calling it. Well, perhaps it will become clearer as we go along. Tell me, we do have arts, don't we?

Gorg. Yes.

Socr. Of all these arts, then, I imagine that some have manufacture as their principal object and need very few words, some none at all, since the production of the art may be effected in complete silence, like painting and sculpture and a good many others. I suppose that is the sort of art you mean when you say rhetoric has no connection with it. Am I right?

Gorg. You catch my meaning quite admirably, Socrates.

Socr. But there are, in fact, other arts which accomplish their entire production through speech, and need either no action at all, so to say, or very little, such as arithmetic and calculation, geometry and chess, and a good many others. In some of them words play almost as much of a part as action and in many even more and—to sum up—their entire activity and effect is produced through words. I think you mean that rhetoric belongs to this class.

Gorg. Quite right.

Socr. But I don't in the least suppose that you want to call any of these arts rhetoric, even though you did imply it by saying that the art whose effect is produced through language is rhetoric. A man who wanted to be unpleasant about the argument might make the assumption: "So you call arithmetic rhetoric, Gorgias?" Still and all, I don't believe you want to call either arithmetic or geometry rhetoric.

451   *Gorg.* Your notion is correct, Socrates, and your supposition justified.

Socr. So let us finish the answer to my question. Since rhetoric is, in fact, one of those arts which make great use of language, but is only one of them, and there are others of this same kind, please try to tell me what it is, in language, upon which rhetoric operates to secure its effect. For example, if some one were to question me about one of the arts I just mentioned: "Socrates, what is the art of arithmetic?" I should tell him, just as you did me, that it was one of the arts whose effect is secured through language. And if he pursued the inquiry: "And with what is it concerned?" I should tell him that it is concerned with odd and even numbers, the complete series of each of them, whatever their amount.

And if he should question me again: "What art do you call calculation?" I should say that it, too, is one of those arts whose total effects are secured through language. And if he returned to the charge: "With reference to what?" I should tell him in the words of those who draft bills for the Assembly,[5] that 'in other respects' calculation is just like arithmetic (it covers the same material, odd and even numbers), yet it differs to this extent, that calculation treats odd and even in respect to their numerical relation both to themselves and to each other. And if the same question were repeated about astronomy, and I replied that this too produces its entire effects by language and my interlocutor asked: "With what is the language of astronomy concerned, Socrates?" I should say that it is concerned with the movements of the stars and the sun and the moon, and with their relative velocity.

Gorg. And you would be quite right, Socrates.

Socr. Come, it's your turn now, Gorgias. We have maintained that rhetoric is one of those arts which accomplish and effect everything through language, haven't we?

Gorg. Right.

Socr. Then tell me what is its subject matter. With what, of all existing things, are the words which rhetoric uses concerned?

Gorg. With the greatest of human concerns, Socrates, and the best.

Socr. But, Gorgias, once again your statement is debatable and as yet by no means clear. I expect you have been present at banquets and heard men singing the drinking song which enumerates that health is best of all, that beauty is second best, and third, according to the author of the song, is to come by honest riches.

Gorg. Yes, I have heard it. But why are you bringing it up?

Socr. Suppose that the producers of these things which the song's author praised, the doctor, the trainer, the businessman, should this instant present themselves before you, and first of all the doctor should say: "Socrates, Gorgias is deceiving you. His art is not concerned with the greatest good for men; it is mine that is." If I were then to ask him: "But who are you to make such claims?" he would be likely to reply that he was a doctor.

452

[5] Referring merely to stereotyped expressions used to avoid repetitions.

"What do you mean? Is the product of your art the greatest good?" "But of course it is, Socrates," he would say. "What greater good have men than health?" And suppose that after him the trainer should come along and say: "I too should be surprised, Socrates, if Gorgias were able to show you a greater good resulting from his art than I can show from mine." I would duly ask him: "And who on earth are you, sir, and what may be your product?" "A trainer," he would say, "and my job is to make men's bodies handsome and strong." And following the trainer the businessman might speak with utter contempt, very possibly, for all the others: "Now think, Socrates, and think well! Does there appear to be a greater good than wealth either in Gorgias' or in anyone else's estimation?" So we should say to him, "What's all this? Are you the producer of this good?" He would answer in the affirmative. "Who are you?" "A businessman." "So you judge wealth to be the greatest good for men?" we should ask. "Of course," he will say. "Yet Gorgias here," we should answer, "maintains that his art is the source of greater good than yours." So obviously his next question will be: "And what is this good? Ask Gorgias to tell us." So come now, Gorgias: Consider yourself to be questioned both by these persons and by me. Tell us what it is that you declare to be the greatest good for mankind and of which you say you are the producer.

Gorg. That, Socrates, which truly is the greatest good and the source, not only of personal freedom for individuals, but also of mastery over others in one's own country.

Socr. Now just what do you mean by that?

Gorg. I mean the ability to persuade with words judges in the law courts, senators in the Senate, assemblymen in the Assembly, and men in any other meeting which convenes for the public interest. Since it is perfectly true that by virtue of this power you will have at your beck and call the physician and the trainer, that businessman of yours will turn out to be making money for somebody else! Not for himself will he make it, but for you who have the power to speak and persuade the vast majority.

Socr. At this moment, Gorgias, you seem to have come very close to defining what sort of art you consider rhetoric to be. If

I understand you at all, you mean that rhetoric produces persuasion. Its entire business is persuasion; the whole sum and substance of it comes to that. Can you, in fact, declare that rhetoric has any further power than to effect persuasion in the listeners' soul?

Gorg. No, I can't, Socrates; you seem to me to be giving an adequate definition. This is really its sum and substance.

Socr. Then listen, Gorgias, for I am quite sure that if there ever was a man who entered on the discussion of a matter from the pure desire to learn the exact truth, I am such a person; and I should say the same about you.

Gorg. Well, what then, Socrates?

Socr. I shall tell you. You must be aware that I have no exact knowledge of what you intend the nature of the persuasion produced by rhetoric to be, or on what objects it functions. Yet, though I have a suspicion of what you mean by that nature and those objects, I shall nevertheless question you about both of these matters. And why do I suppress my suspicions and question you instead of speaking up myself? It is not really for your sake, but for that of the argument, in order that it may advance with both of us being informed as clearly as possible about the matters under discussion. Do you think I am right in continuing to question you? If, for example, I were questioning you about what class of painters Zeuxis belonged to and you told me he was a figure-painter, don't you think I should be right to question you about what sort of figures he painted?

Gorg. Of course.

Socr. And right for this reason: there are many other figure-painters who paint many other kinds of figures?

Gorg. Yes.

Socr. But if no one but Zeuxis were painting, you would have made a good reply?

Gorg. Right.

Socr. Go on then and tell me about rhetoric. Do you think rhetoric is the only art to produce persuasion? May other arts do it also? I mean something of this sort: When a man teaches anything, is his teaching persuasion or is it not?

Gorg. But of course he persuades, Socrates; why, certainly he does.

Socr. In that case we must return to the arts we just finished discussing. Don't arithmetic and the arithmetician teach us the properties of number?

Gorg. To be sure.

Socr. So the arithmetician persuades also?

Gorg. Yes.

Socr. Then arithmetic is a producer of persuasion?

Gorg. It seems to be.

Socr. Then, if anyone questions us about what sort of persuasion is intended and what its object may be, we shall presumably answer him that it is of the sort that provides instruction about the odd and the even and their quantities. And in the case of all the other arts we mentioned just now, we shall be able to prove that they produce persuasion and what sort of persuasion they produce and in regard to what class of objects. Is this true?

454

Gorg. Yes.

Socr. Then rhetoric is not the only producer of persuasion.

Gorg. That is so.

Socr. Since, therefore, rhetoric is not the only art producing this effect, but there are others also which may do so, we shall be justified in questioning further anyone who makes this affirmation, as we did in the case of the painter: Of what sort of persuasion in regard to what object is rhetoric the art? Don't you think that this additional question is justified?

Gorg. I do.

Socr. Answer it, then, Gorgias, since you too hold the same views.

Gorg. Very well. The sort of persuasion I mean, Socrates, is the kind used in law courts and other public gatherings, as I said just a moment ago, and it deals with justice and injustice.

Socr. I, too, suspected, as you must know, Gorgias, that this was the kind of persuasion and these were the objects you meant. But do not be surprised if presently I ask you the sort of question the answer to which seems obvious, but which I still insist on repeating. This I do to complete the argument in an orderly way and not to discredit you. It is better that we should not habitually suspect each other's meaning and anticipate statements. Another purpose is that you may round out your views just as you see fit, in accordance with your true aim.

Gorg. This certainly seems to be the correct procedure, Socrates.

Socr. Well then, let us examine the following point: Is there such a thing as 'to have learned'?

Gorg. There is.

Socr. And 'to believe'?

Gorg. Yes.

Socr. Then do you think that to have learned is the same as to believe? That is, is knowledge the same as belief or are they different?

Gorg. To my mind, Socrates, they seem different.

Socr. You are quite right and you may confirm your opinion from this fact: If anyone should ask you, "Gorgias, is there such a thing as a false belief and a true belief?" I imagine that you would say that there is.

Gorg. Yes.

Socr. Well then, is there both a false and a true knowledge?

Gorg. Certainly not.

Socr. Then it is perfectly clear that knowledge and belief are not the same.

Gorg. True.

Socr. Still, those who have learned have been persuaded just as much as those who believe.

Gorg. That is so.

Socr. Shall we, then, assume two kinds of persuasion, the one producing belief without certainty, the other knowledge?

Gorg. Yes, of course.

Socr. Then which kind of persuasion concerning justice and injustice does rhetoric effect in law courts and other public gatherings, the kind which produces belief without knowledge, or the kind which yields knowledge?

Gorg. It would seem quite obvious, Socrates, that it is the kind which produces mere belief.

Socr. So rhetoric, it seems, effects a persuasion which can produce belief about justice and injustice, but cannot give instruction about them.

Gorg. Yes.

Socr. The rhetorician, then, is not a teacher of law courts and other public gatherings as to what is right or wrong, but merely a creator of beliefs; for evidently he could never instruct so large a gathering on such weighty matters in a short time.

Gorg. He certainly couldn't.

Socr. Come then, let us see what it may be that we mean by rhetoric; for myself, as you see, I have not yet been able to formulate what I do mean. On occasions when the city holds a meeting for the purpose of electing state-physicians or shipwrights or any other kind of master-worker, surely the rhetorician will then refrain from giving his advice? For obviously in all cases like this it is imperative to elect the ablest craftsman. And when walls are to be built, or harbors or docks to be constructed, not the rhetorician but the master-builders will give advice. And again, when counsel is needed about the choice of generals or the disposition of troops against the enemy, or the occupation of hostile territory, military experts will give the advice, not rhetoricians. Or what would you say about such cases, Gorgias? Since you profess yourself to be an orator and to qualify others as speakers, it is only proper to learn from you what pertains to your art. Now consider that I too am concerned to promote your interests, for some of the people present may very well desire to become your pupil. I suspect, in fact, that there are not a few who may have this desire and yet are, perhaps, shy about asking you questions. So when I question you, consider that you are being interrogated by them also. "What benefit shall we have, Gorgias, if we attend your lectures? What are the matters in which we shall be able to advise the State? Justice and injustice alone, or those other matters also which Socrates just mentioned?" So try, please, to give them an answer.

Gorg. Well, Socrates, I shall try to reveal to you clearly the entire power of rhetoric; you, in fact, courteously pointed out the way yourself. You know, of course, that these docks and walls of

Athens and the construction of the harbors proceeded from the counsel of Themistocles and, in part, Pericles, not from mere craftsmen.

Socr. So they say, Gorgias, about Themistocles; as for Pericles, I myself was present and heard him when he gave us advice about the Middle Wall.

Gorg. And so you see, Socrates, that whenever there is an election to posts such as those you have just mentioned, it is the orators who give advice and whose opinions win the day.

456

Socr. It is because this is so astonishing, Gorgias, that I have now long been asking what on earth this power of rhetoric can be. When I examine its vast proportions, it seems to me little short of supernatural.

Gorg. Ah, Socrates, if only you knew the whole of it! How it embraces, so to say, all the other arts! I shall give you an important proof of this. On many occasions in the past, in the company of my brother and other physicians, I have made calls on patients who were unwilling to take their medicine or submit to an operation or a cautery; and though their doctor could not persuade them, I did so, by no other art than rhetoric. And I make the further declaration that if a rhetorician and a physician should come to any city you please and have occasion to debate in the assembly or any other public gathering as to which of them ought to be elected public physician, the doctor would be utterly eclipsed, and the capable speaker would, if he chose, be elected. And likewise in a contest with any other craftsman whatsoever, the rhetorician would win his own election against all opposition of any kind; for not a single craftsman is able to speak in a crowd, on any subject in the world, more persuasively than the rhetorician. This is to show you how great and how splendid is the power of his art.

One should, however, Socrates, make use of rhetoric in the same way as one does of every other sort of proficiency. This, too, one should not employ against any and everybody. Because a man has learned to be so proficient in boxing or wrestling or the use of arms that he is superior to friend and foe alike, that is no reason for him to go about beating or stabbing and killing his

friends! And if a man frequents the gymnasia, gets his body in
first rate condition, becomes a prize-fighter, and then takes to
beating his father and mother or his friends and relatives, that
is no reason for detesting and banishing the trainers and teachers
of the art of fighting! You can recognize that they imparted their
instruction to be used rightly in self-defense against enemies and
criminals; but the pupils perverted their own strength and skill
to its wrong use. The teachers, therefore, are not evil, nor is their
art responsible for these misdeeds, nor is it vicious in itself; those
who misuse the art I hold to be responsible.

Exactly the same argument holds for rhetoric also. The rhetorician is capable of speaking against everyone else and on any
subject you please in such a way that he can win over vast multitudes to anything, in a word, that he may desire. But the fact
that he can rob doctors, or any other craftsmen, of the credit due
them, is no reason why he should do so: he must use his skill justly,
exactly as one should physical prowess. And if a man learns rhetoric, and then does injustice through the power of his art, we
shall not be right, in my opinion, in detesting and banishing his
teacher. For while the teacher imparted instruction to be used
rightly, the pupil made a contrary use of it. Therefore it is only
right to detest the misuser and banish and kill him, not his teacher.

Socr. I imagine, Gorgias, that you, too, have taken part in
many discussions and have discovered in the course of them this
peculiar situation arising: people do not find it easy by an exchange of views to arrive at a mutually satisfactory definition
for the subjects under discussion, and in this way bring the argument to an agreeable end. Rather, when they disagree on any
point, and one declares the other to be guilty of incorrect or
vague statements, they grow angry and imagine that everything
that is said proceeds from ill will, not from any concern about
the matters under discussion. Some of these arguments end most
disgracefully, breaking up in mutual vituperation to such an extent that the bystanders are annoyed at themselves for having
become auditors of such people. Now why do I say this? Because
at the moment you seem to me to be making statements which
do not follow from, and are not consistent with, what you first

said about rhetoric. I hesitate, therefore, to embark on a refutation in the fear that you may imagine that I am speaking, not with a view to illuminating our subject, but to discredit you. Now if you are the sort of person I am, I shall gladly continue the questions and answers; if not, I shall let them go. And what sort of person am I? One of those who are happy to be refuted if they make a false statement, happy also to refute anyone else who may do the same, yet not less happy to be refuted than to refute. For I think the former a greater benefit, in proportion as it is of greater benefit to be oneself delivered from the greatest harm than to deliver another. No worse harm, it is true, can befall a man than to hold wrong opinions on the matters now under discussion between us. If, then, you declare yourself to be such a person as I am, let us continue the discussion; but if you think we ought to let it go, let us at once dismiss it and close the interview.

Gorg. But I do indeed nominate myself, Socrates, to be just such a person as you describe. Perhaps, however, we ought to give some consideration to the others here with us. For quite some time, you know, even before you came in, I had been delivering a long address to the company here; and now, perhaps, if we continue our discussion, it may be somewhat protracted. We should, then, consider whether we are not detaining some of the others who may wish to attend to some other business.

Chaer. You may judge from the applause, Gorgias and Socrates, that these gentlemen are eager to hear whatever you have to say. What I can certainly do is to speak for myself: I trust I may never be so pressed for time as to relinquish such an argument and one so well handled in the belief that anything else in the world is more advantageous.

Call. Yes, Chaerephon, I'll be bound I too have been present at many an argument, but not once did I ever enjoy myself as I'm doing now. As far as I'm concerned, if you want to go on talking the entire day, you'll only be doing me a favor.

Socr. Well, Callicles, from my point of view there's nothing to prevent it, if Gorgias is agreeable.

Gorg. After all this, Socrates, it would certainly be disgraceful

458

for me alone not to be agreeable, especially since I've already declared that anyone may ask any question he desires. So, if that's what everyone here wants, continue the discourse and ask anything you like.

Socr. Then let me tell you, Gorgias, what surprises me in your remarks. It is possible, of course, that I misunderstood what you stated quite correctly. Do you declare that you are able to make a rhetorician out of anyone who comes to you to learn?

Gorg. Yes.

Socr. Do you mean, capable of winning over a crowd on any subject whatever, not by instruction, but by persuasion?

459   *Gorg.* Quite so.

Socr. I believe you said just now that the orator will be more persuasive than the physician even on the subject of health.

Gorg. Yes, but I added 'in a crowd.'

Socr. Then the qualification 'in a crowd' means 'among the ignorant'? For surely the orator will not be more persuasive than the doctor among those who really know.

Gorg. That is true.

Socr. And so, if he is to be more persuasive than the doctor, he becomes more persuasive than one who really knows?

Gorg. Surely.

Socr. Though he is not a doctor himself? Is this true?

Gorg. Yes.

Socr. And one who is not a doctor is, of course, ignorant of a doctor's knowledge?

Gorg. Obviously.

Socr. So when the rhetorician is more persuasive than the doctor, it is a case of the ignorant being more persuasive than the expert in the company of the ignorant. Is that the way of it or is it not?

Gorg. That is, of course, the way of it in this case.

Socr. Moreover, the rhetorician and his rhetoric will have the same relation to all the other arts: there is no need for rhetoric to know the facts at all, for it has hit upon a means of persuasion that enables it to appear, in the eyes of the ignorant, to know more than those who really know.

Gorg. Well, Socrates, isn't that a delightfully easy way of doing things: to make oneself a match for the experts in the other arts, though one has learned none of them, only this one?

Socr. Whether the rhetorician is, or is not, a match for the others through this state of affairs we may examine later if it appears material to our argument. For the moment let us rather consider this point: Is the rhetorician's equipment the same in regard to justice and injustice, beauty and ugliness, good and evil, as it is regarding health and the several subjects of the other arts? Is it, in fact, true that he does not really know what is good or evil, beautiful or ugly, just or unjust, but has devised a means of persuasion about them so that, in the eyes of the ignorant, he seems to know more than the actual possessor of knowledge though he does not really do so? Or is it necessary for him to know? Must the man who intends to learn rhetoric have acquired this knowledge before he comes to you? And if he hasn't, will you, the teacher of rhetoric, teach him none of these things (of course that's not really your job), but instead will you make him, in the eyes of the crowd, seem to know such things, though he doesn't, and seem to be good, though he isn't? Or is it a fact that you will not be able to teach him rhetoric at all until he first learns the truth about these matters? What is really the situation in such cases, Gorgias? For heaven's sake, strip the veil off rhetoric, as you promised to do, and tell us what on earth its power may be!

Gorg. Why, Socrates, it is my opinion that if a pupil does not happen to know these things, he will learn them, as well as rhetoric, from me.

Socr. Good! Stop there! What a splendid thing to say! If you are going to make a man a rhetorician, he must know justice and injustice; he must either have acquired this knowledge previously or have learned it subsequently from you.

Gorg. Quite so.

Socr. What follows now? Is a man who has learned the art of building a builder, or is he not?

Gorg. He is.

Socr. And likewise a man who has learned music is a musician?

Gorg. Yes.

Socr. And a man who has mastered medicine, a doctor? And so on, according to the same principle: does everyone who has learned an art acquire that character which is imparted to him by the knowledge of it?

Gorg. Quite so.

Socr. And so, on this principle, the man who has learned justice is a just man?

Gorg. Most assuredly.

Socr. And, being just, may be presumed to act justly?

Gorg. Yes.

Socr. Then it follows that the rhetorician will be just, inasmuch as a just man will wish to act justly.

Gorg. It would seem so.

[*Socr.* And that the just man will never wish to do wrong?

Gorg. That is so.

Socr. And the argument indicates that the rhetorician must be just?

Gorg. Yes.

Socr. Never, consequently, will the rhetorician wish to do injustice?

Gorg. It seems that he will not.] [6]

Socr. Well then, do you remember saying a little while ago that one should not blame trainers or banish them if the boxer-pupil makes a perverted use of his art and commits unjust acts? And in the same way if the orator makes a wrong use of his rhetoric we ought not to blame or expel his teacher, but inflict this punishment on the wrong-doer who has made an improper use of his art? Was this the statement you made or was it not?

Gorg. It was.

Socr. But now, as it seems, this same person, the rhetorician, could not ever have committed injustice. Right?

Gorg. So it seems.

Socr. And there is the further fact, Gorgias, that in our preliminary discussion it was affirmed that rhetoric was concerned

[6] The bracketed passage is probably an interpolation.

with statements, not about odd or even, but about justice and injustice. Is that true?

Gorg. Yes.

Socr. Consequently I assumed, when you made this statement, that rhetoric could never be anything unjust, since its propositions are always about justice. So when, a little later, you said that the orator might make use of rhetoric for unjust purposes also, I was astonished and, believing that these assertions were inconsistent, I made the statement that, if you were like me and believed refutation to be an advantage, it was worth while to continue the discussion; but if you did not, we had better dismiss the subject. And later, when we resumed the inquiry, you see yourself that we have once again agreed that it is impossible for the rhetorician to use his art unjustly or wish to commit injustice. So, Gorgias, by the Dog, god of the Egyptians, to sift this subject adequately and see where matters really stand will need a very considerable colloquy.

461

Pol. How's that, Socrates? Do you really believe yourself what you're saying about rhetoric? Or do you think because Gorgias was ashamed not to admit to you that a man versed in rhetoric didn't also know justice and beauty and goodness and, if he came for instruction without this knowledge, that he would teach him himself—and then from this admission a little inconsistency, perhaps, crept into the argument [7]—that's a thing you love to do, turning the argument to questions like this—for who do you think would ever deny that Gorgias understands justice and can teach others? It's just downright rude to turn the argument to such questions!

Socr. My excellent Polus, there you have it. The very reason we seek to acquire children and friends is this: When we get on in years and make mistakes, they will be at our side with youthful vigor to correct the way we comport ourselves, both in words and in deeds. So now, if Gorgias or myself has made any slip in our argument, here you are to set us straight. And it's only right that you should. For my part, I shall be delighted to retract any conclusion that may seem wrong, if you'll be kind enough to observe just one little rule.

[7] Polus, in his indignation, discards all pretence to formal grammar.

Pol. What do you mean?

Socr. If, Polus, you will keep a tight rein upon your discursiveness, which you tried to indulge in the first instance.

Pol. How's that? Am I not to be allowed to say as much as I please?

Socr. It would indeed be a dreadful experience for you, my dear fellow, to come to Athens, where there is the greatest freedom of speech, and be the only one denied this privilege. But just look at the other side: If you insist on making long speeches and refuse to answer questions, wouldn't it be an equally dreadful experience for me if I were not to have the privilege of going away to avoid listening to you? If you have any feeling for the discussion we have been undertaking and wish to set it straight, do as I have just suggested: take back any point you like and in turn, through question and answer, present your refutation or be refuted, just as Gorgias and I have been doing. You are, of course, asserting that you have cognizance of all that Gorgias knows. Am I right?

Pol. You are.

Socr. So then I suppose that you, like him, urge all of us to ask you any question we wish, with the assurance that you know how to give the right answer?

Pol. Certainly, certainly.

Socr. Then, choose whichever course you wish to follow: to ask or to answer.

Pol. I'll do the asking. So answer me this, Socrates! Since you think Gorgias is at a loss about rhetoric, what do you say it is?

Socr. Are you asking what sort of an art I say it is?

Pol. I am.

Socr. Well, to tell you the honest truth, Polus, it doesn't seem to me to be any sort of art.

Pol. Then what do you think rhetoric is?

Socr. A thing which you claim to have made an art in that treatise I recently read.

Pol. What thing do you mean?

Socr. A kind of knack.

Pol. So rhetoric seems to you to be a knack?

Socr. It does, unless you have some other term to suggest.

Pol. A knack of what?

Socr. Of producing a certain kind of gratification and pleasure.

Pol. Then doesn't rhetoric seem to you to be a fine thing, being capable of giving men pleasure?

Socr. How do you mean, Polus? Have you already so thoroughly learned from me what I say rhetoric is that you can ask the next question: "Don't you think it is fine?"

Pol. Well, haven't I learned that you say it's a knack?

Socr. Will you be so kind, since you set such value on pleasure, to give me a little?

Pol. Of course.

Socr. Ask me, then, what sort of an art, in my opinion, is cookery?

Pol. All right, I'm asking. What art is cookery?

Socr. None at all, Polus.

Pol. Then what is it? Tell me.

Socr. I say that it is a certain knack.

Pol. A knack of what, if you please?

Socr. I say a knack of producing gratification and pleasure, Polus.

Pol. So cooking and rhetoric are the same thing?

Socr. Not at all; both are branches of the same pursuit.

Pol. And what may that be?

Socr. I hope it isn't rude to speak the truth. It is for Gorgias' sake that I hesitate to continue, for fear he may think that I'm ridiculing his profession. I don't really know whether this is the rhetoric which Gorgias professes (from our recent discussion no clear notion of what he does think it is has emerged); yet this is what I call rhetoric, a branch of a thing which has nothing 'fine' about it at all.

463

Gorg. What thing, Socrates? Tell us, please, and don't worry about me!

Socr. Well then, to me, Gorgias, rhetoric seems not to be an artistic pursuit at all, but that of a shrewd, courageous spirit which is naturally clever at dealing with men; and I call the chief part of it flattery. It seems to me to have many branches and one of them is cookery, which is thought to be an art, but according to

my notion is no art at all, but a knack and a routine. I hold that
rhetoric, too, is a branch of this pursuit, and so is make-up [8] and
sophistic—four branches applied to four different things. If, then,
Polus wants to find this out, let him question me. For, as it is, he
has not yet learned what branch of flattery I call rhetoric; for-
getting that I haven't answered this yet, he goes on to ask me if I
don't think it is fine. I shall not answer whether I think rhetoric is
fine or foul until he first asks me what it is. You're not being fair,
Polus. Yet, if you wish to discover my views, ask me what branch
of flattery rhetoric is.

Pol. All right, I'll ask. Tell me which branch.

Socr. Will you, I wonder, be any the wiser for my answer?
Rhetoric, in my account, is a reflection of a branch of politics.

Pol. Oh? Then do you call it fine or foul?

Socr. I call it foul, as I do all ugly things, since I have to answer you as though you had already grasped my meaning.

Gorg. But, good heavens, Socrates, I myself don't follow your
drift.

Socr. Surely, that's only natural, Gorgias, for I haven't yet been
able to present anything clearly. Polus [9] here is young and full of
high spirits.

Gorg. Well, never mind him. Tell me what you mean when you
say that rhetoric is the reflection of a branch of politics.

Socr. Yes, I will try to tell you what to me, at least, rhetoric
seems to be; and if I miss the mark, Polus here shall show me up.
I suppose you call 'body' something and 'soul' something else?

Gorg. Surely.

Socr. Then for each of them you think there is such a thing as
good conditioning?

Gorg. I do.

Socr. Well, is there such a thing as a condition which seems to
be good, but really isn't? Here's an illustration of what I mean:
there are many people who seem to be in such good health that
it isn't easy for anyone except a physician or a trainer to perceive
that they are not.

---

[8] Or, as it is elegantly styled today, 'the art of the beautician.'
[9] POLUS, in Greek, means 'colt.'

Gorg. That's true.

Socr. I affirm that some such condition may be present both in soul and in body, which makes them both seem to be healthy when, in fact, they are not.

Gorg. That also is true.

Socr. Now let me, if I may, show you more clearly what I mean. Since this natural duality exists, I assume two arts to correspond to it. That which presides over the soul I call politics; to that which governs the body I cannot give a single name; yet, since the care of the body is a single art, I call its two branches gymnastics and medicine. In politics as against gymnastics I place legislation, and that which is the counterpart of medicine I call justice. Both of these pairs have a good deal in common, medicine with gymnastics, and justice with legislation—naturally, for they preside over the same object; nonetheless they have some differences from each other. Now of these four, which always have the greatest good of the soul or the body in view, the art of flattery takes note—I won't say with full knowledge, but by shrewd guessing—and divides herself into four, entering secretly into each of the branches, and pretends that she has become what she has entered, caring nothing for the greatest good, but seeking to entrap ignorance with the bait of the pleasure of the moment. And she accomplishes her deceitful design to the extent that she has come to be considered of the highest value. In this way, then, cookery has smuggled herself into the guise of medicine, and pretends she knows which foods are best for the body; so that if a cook and a physician had to dispute their claims before a group of boys, or before men as silly as boys, as to which of the two completely understood which foods are beneficial and which are harmful, the physician would starve to death. Now I call this flattery, and I say that such a proceeding is foul, Polus—I am addressing this directly to you—because it aims at pleasure without consideration of what is best; and I say that it is not an art, but a knack, because it is unable to render any account of the nature of the methods it applies and so cannot tell the cause of each of them. I am unable to give the name of art to anything irrational; but if

465

you contest any of these statements, I am ready to be cross-examined.[10]

Socr. (continuing) So, as I say, the flattery of cooking has taken the guise of medicine; and the pretence of gymnastics has been assumed in this same way by the flattery of make-up, a thing evil and deceitful, ignoble and illiberal, performing its deceptions by means of forms and colors, polish and fine garments, assuming a borrowed beauty to the neglect of natural loveliness which comes only through gymnastics. Well, not to make too long a tale of it, I'll put it in geometrical form (for by this time you are surely following my drift): as make-up is to gymnastics, so is sophistic to legislation; and as cookery to medicine, so is rhetoric to justice. As I have said, however, though there is this natural distinction between them, yet because they are closely related and deal with the same matters, sophists and rhetoricians become confused and do not know either what to make of themselves nor do others know what to make of them. In fact, if the soul were not in charge of the body, if the body were in its own charge and not monitored by the soul to distinguish cookery and medicine, if it were left by itself to estimate them by the gratification provided, the dictum of Anaxagoras would prevail far and wide, my dear Polus (you, of course, are an expert in this field): everything would be jumbled together and we should not be able to distinguish medicinal and healthy concoctions from those of cookery. Now you have heard what I say rhetoric is: the counterpart of cookery in the soul, as cookery is its counterpart in the body.

Well, perhaps I've done an absurd thing in not permitting you to make a long speech, while holding forth at some length myself. Yet you really must forgive me, for when I gave brief answers, you didn't understand them; nor were you able to make any use of my rejoinders, but required a thorough exposition. So if I, in my turn, am unable to make proper use of your answers, don't hesitate to prolong the exposition; but if I can make use of them, let me do so. That is only fair. And now, if you want to make any use of this answer of mine, please do so.

466

10 There is a dramatic pause here, while Polus fidgets.

Pol. So this is your answer, that rhetoric seems to you to be flattery?

Socr. No. I said a branch of flattery. What a memory you have for your years, Polus! What will become of you by and by?

Pol. Then is it your opinion that good orators are esteemed to be worthless flatterers in their own country?

Socr. Do you ask this as a question or as the beginning of an exposition?

Pol. It's a question that I'm asking.

Socr. Then, in my opinion, they aren't esteemed at all.

Pol. Not esteemed! Don't they have the greatest power in the country?

Socr. No; if, at least, by 'power' you mean something good to the man who wields it.

Pol. That, of course, is my meaning.

Socr. Then, in my opinion, orators have the least power of any of their fellow citizens.

Pol. What's this? Don't they act like tyrants and put to death any one they please and confiscate property and banish any one they've a mind to?

Socr. By the Dog, Polus, I can't make up my mind whether every word you say is a statement of your own opinion, or whether you're asking me a question.

Pol. But of course I'm asking you.

Socr. Well, well, dear boy; so you want to ask me two questions at the same time?

Pol. How do you mean, two?

Socr. Didn't you just say something of this sort: "Don't the orators put to death any one they please, just like tyrants, and confiscate property and banish any one they've a mind to?"

Pol. I did.

Socr. I tell you, then, that these questions of yours are two, and yet I'll give you an answer to both of them. I assert, Polus, that both orators and tyrants have the least possible power in their own countries, as I said just now. For they do nothing, so to speak, that they wish to do, and yet do what is in their opinion best.

Pol. Well, isn't that having great power?

Socr. Not, at least, according to Polus.

Pol. I say it isn't? But I say it is!

Socr. Now I swear by—! But you don't really, since you said great power was a good to the man who controls it.

Pol. Yes, and I do say so.

Socr. So you think it is good for a man without sense to do what he thinks is best for him? And you call this great power?

Pol. Of course I don't.

Socr. Then won't you have to refute me? Won't you have to prove that the orators have sense and that rhetoric is an art and not mere flattery? If you leave me unrefuted, the orators and tyrants who do what they think best in their several countries will get no good from it; and even if power, as you claim, were a good thing, to have no sense and yet do what one thinks best, even you admit to be bad. Am I right?

Pol. Right.

Socr. Then how can orators or tyrants have great power if Socrates is not forced by Polus to acknowledge that they do what they really wish to do?

Pol. This fellow—

Socr. I deny that they do what they wish. Now refute me!

Pol. Weren't you just now admitting that they do what seems best to them?

Socr. And, moreover, I admit it now.

Pol. Then don't they do what they wish?

Socr. Not according to me.

Pol. Yet they do what seems best to them?

Socr. I agree.

Pol. Socrates, the things you say are dreadful, they are monstrous!

Socr. Don't scold me, please, most polished of Poluses, if I may address you in your own style.[11] If you want to question me and show that I'm wrong, do so; if not, prepare to answer questions yourself.

---

[11] That is, in a jingle of more or less meaningless sounds, as illustrated in Polus' speech above (p. 5).

Pol. Well, I'm willing to do the answering, if only to find out what you really do mean.

Socr. Is it your opinion, then, that men desire the action they perform? Or do they desire the object of this action? For example do you think that men who take medicine on a doctor's prescription desire the action, the drinking of the medicine and the consequent discomfort, or do they desire health and it is for this reason that they take the medicine?

Pol. Obviously health.

Socr. So also in the case of merchants and traders who go to sea, what they desire is not what they do (for who would choose the dangers and discomforts of a long sea voyage?); but what they want, I suppose, is the object of their voyage, to get rich; and it is for the sake of wealth that they go to sea.

Pol. Quite so.

Socr. And isn't the same true in all other cases? When a man engages in an action for the sake of something else, it is not the action he desires, but the end and object of the action?

Pol. Yes.

Socr. Is there, then, any existing thing which is not either good or bad, or is between these extremes, being neither good nor bad?

Pol. There couldn't be, Socrates.

Socr. Then do you call wisdom and health and wealth and everything else of this sort good and their opposites bad?

Pol. I do.

Socr. And the things that are neither good nor bad, would you say that they are of the sort that sometimes has elements of good, sometimes of bad, sometimes of neither, things like sitting down and walking and running and sailing or, to choose a different kind of example, stones and wood and things of that nature? You mean this sort of thing, don't you? Or would you give the term 'neither good nor bad' to any other class of things?

Pol. No, these are what I mean.

Socr. Then when people perform these neutral actions, do they perform them for the sake of the good, or do good for the sake of the neutral?

468

Pol. Of course, they act in this neutral manner for the sake of the good.

Socr. So it is in pursuit of the good that we walk when we walk, believing that to be the better course at the moment; and, contrariwise, stand still when we do stand still, with the same object in view, the good? Right?

Pol. Yes.

Socr. And likewise, if we ever have occasion to put a man to death or banish him and confiscate his property, do we do this in the belief that we are benefiting ourselves from such actions? Or don't we?

Pol. We do.

Socr. So it is for the sake of the good that people who do all these things take these actions?

Pol. Yes, it is.

Socr. And we have admitted that when we act for any purpose, we do not desire the action itself, but the object of the action?

Pol. To be sure.

Socr. Then we do not desire to kill or banish or confiscate—not the simple actions themselves; but if they are advantageous, we desire to do them; and if they are harmful, we do not. For we desire what is good, as you affirm; but things that are neither bad nor good we do not desire, nor things that are bad, either. Well, does my statement seem to you to be correct, Polus? Why don't you answer?

Pol. Correct.

Socr. Then, in view of these admissions, if a man, whether a tyrant or an orator, kills or banishes or confiscates, in the belief that it is to his advantage, when it really is to his disadvantage, he, I presume, is doing what seems best to him. Right?

Pol. Yes.

Socr. Then does he also do what he desires, even if his actions are bad for him? Why don't you answer?

Pol. No, I don't think he does what he desires.

Socr. Is it, then, possible to say that such a man has great power in his country? If, that is, great power is something good, according to your admission?

Pol. It is not possible.

Socr. So I was right in saying that a man may do what seems best to him and yet neither have great power in his own country nor do what he desires.

Pol. Just exactly as though you, Socrates, would not choose to have the power to do what you thought best rather than not to have it! Just as though you wouldn't feel envy if you saw another man who had killed anyone he pleased, or robbed him, or put him in prison!

Socr. Do you mean justly or unjustly?

Pol. Whichever it may be, isn't it enviable either way?

Socr. Hush, hush, my dear Polus!

Pol. What's the matter?

Socr. We must never envy the unenviable or the wretched, but pity them.

Pol. How's that? Is this your opinion of the condition of the men I mentioned?

Socr. How could it be otherwise?

Pol. So whoever kills, and justly kills, anyone he judges proper seems to you to be wretched and pitiable?

Socr. No, but scarcely enviable.

Pol. But didn't you just say that he was wretched?

Socr. No, my friend, I was talking about the man who killed unjustly, and he is pitiable as well; but a man who kills justly is still unenviable.

Pol. Well, at any rate, there's no doubt that a man who is put to death unjustly is really pitiable and wretched.

Socr. Less so than the man who kills him, Polus, and also less than the man who is put to death justly.

Pol. Now what on earth do you mean by that, Socrates?

Socr. That to do injustice is the greatest of all evils.

Pol. What? Is it the greatest? Isn't to suffer injustice a greater evil?

Socr. By no means.

Pol. So you'd prefer to suffer injustice rather than do it?

Socr. For myself I should prefer neither; but if it were neces-

469

sary for me either to do or to suffer injustice, I should choose to
suffer rather than do it.

Pol. So I suppose you wouldn't like to become a tyrant?

Socr. Certainly not, if you mean by that what I do.

Pol. Well, I mean by it what I said just now, the ability to do
whatever a man pleases: to kill and banish and do everything according to his own fancy.

Socr. And now, my dear friend, let me talk for a bit; then attack me! Imagine that I'm in the crowded market place with a
dagger concealed under my arm and I say to you, "Polus, I have
just acquired an amazing sort of tyrannic power. If I think that
any one of these men whom you see here ought to die this very instant, die he shall, whomever I choose! And if I think that any
of their heads should be bashed in, bashed it shall be right on the
spot! Or if a coat should be slit, slit it shall be! That's the sort of
power I hold in this city!" Then if you didn't believe me and I
showed you my dagger, you might look at it and say, "Why
Socrates, everybody can have that sort of power. In this way you
might burn down any house you pleased, and even the Athenian
dockyards and the men-of-war and all the ships, both public and
private." But surely this is not what one means by having great
power: to do anything one pleases. Do you agree?

Pol. Emphatically, it is not.

470   *Socr.* Can you tell me, then, why you disapprove of power of
this kind?

Pol. I can.

Socr. What is the reason? Tell me, please.

Pol. Because punishment is the inevitable consequence of such
actions.

Socr. And punishment is a bad thing?

Pol. Very bad.

Socr. Well, my elusive friend, you seem to have come around
again to the opinion that if one does as one pleases and the consequences are advantageous, it is a good thing, and that this alone,
so it appears, is great power; if not, it is both bad and weak. But
let us consider this point also: shall we admit that sometimes it is
better to commit these acts we have just mentioned, to kill and

banish human beings and confiscate their property, and that sometimes it is not?

Pol. Certainly.

Socr. It seems, then, that this is really a joint admission on both our parts.

Pol. Yes.

Socr. Now on what occasions do you claim it is better to commit these acts? Tell me where you draw the line.

Pol. Now, Socrates, suppose you answer the question.

Socr. Well, then I say, Polus, if you'd rather hear it from me, that it's better when the action is just, and worse when unjust.

Pol. They say it's hard to refute you, Socrates; but even a child could prove that what you're saying now is false.

Socr. In that case I shall be very much obliged to the child, and equally obliged to you as well, if you will kindly disprove me and rid me of my nonsense. Please do not grow weary in well-doing toward your friend. Refute me!

Pol. Well really, Socrates, there's no need to go back into ancient history for the refutation. Plenty of things have happened yesterday and the day before to show you up and prove that many men who do evil are quite happy.

Socr. What sort of things do you mean?

Pol. I presume you are able to see that Archelaus, son of Perdiccas, is king of Macedonia?

Socr. Well, if I can't, at least I have heard so.

Pol. Do you think he's happy or wretched?

Socr. I haven't the remotest notion, Polus. I've never met the man.

Pol. How's that? You could tell if you met him, but otherwise you don't know instinctively that he's a happy man?

Socr. No, I really don't.

Pol. Well, then it's quite obvious, Socrates, that you're going to say that you don't know whether even the king of Persia is happy!

Socr. And I rather think I should be right: I know nothing about his education or his attitude toward justice.

Pol. How's that? Is this what all of happiness consists in?

Socr. According to my account it is, Polus. I call a good and honorable man or woman happy, and one who is unjust and evil wretched.

471   *Pol.* So Archelaus is wretched, according to you?

Socr. Yes, dear friend, if he is really unjust.

Pol. But how can he be other than unjust? Not a bit of the power he now holds was his by right. He was born from a slave woman of Perdiccas' brother Alcetas and so by rights he was Alcetas' slave; and if he had wanted to act justly, he would still be his slave—and happy, according to your account! But as it is, it's quite amazing how wretched he has become, since he has been guilty of the gravest acts of injustice. The first thing he did was send for his own master, his uncle, under the pretext of restoring him to the power which Perdiccas had usurped. Well, he entertained Alcetas and his son, Alexander, his own cousin, a boy about the same age as himself, got them drunk, threw them into a wagon, drove them off into the night, cut their throats, and no one ever saw them again!

And when he had committed this crime, quite unaware that he had become the most wretched of men, he experienced no repentance. He had a brother, the legitimate son of Perdiccas, a child about seven years old, to whom the kingdom belonged by rights; so a little later, not wishing to become happy or to bring up his brother in accordance with justice or to give him back his kingdom, he threw him into a well and drowned him, telling the mother Cleopatra that the boy had been pursuing a goose when he fell in and died. So now, since he is the greatest criminal in Macedonia, Archelaus is the most wretched of the Macedonians, not the happiest! I daresay there are plenty of Athenians, beginning with you, who would be willing to take the place of any other Macedonian whatever, rather than be Archelaus.

Socr. At the very beginning of our conversation, Polus, I praised you because you seemed to me to be well grounded in rhetoric, though I thought you had neglected dialectic. So now this is the famous argument, is it, by which even a child could refute me? And am I now, in your opinion, refuted by this argument when I declare that the wrongdoer is unhappy? How can this be, my friend? For I don't acknowledge as valid a single one of your premises.

Pol. You don't because you don't want to; and yet you really believe just as I say.

Socr. My gifted friend, you say this because you are attempting to refute me in the rhetorical way, as they fancy they do in the law courts. And it is a fact that there one party is supposed to refute the other by introducing many reputable witnesses to the truth of the statements, whereas the opponent is able to offer only one or none at all. But this sort of proof is valueless in the pursuit of truth; it may even happen sometimes that a man is defeated by scores of false witnesses of apparent respectability. So now, in the present case, nearly everybody, Athenians and foreigners alike, will agree with you, if you want to introduce witnesses against me and the truth of what I say. You may have, if you like, the testimony of Nicias, the son of Niceratus, and his brothers too, whose votive tripods stand row on row in the Dionysium; or, if you like, Aristocrates, the son of Scellias, the donor of that beautiful offering at Delphi; or you may have the entire household of Pericles or any other family at Athens you care to choose. I alone stand out against you, and you will not force me down though you bring clouds of false witnesses against me to dislodge me from my stronghold, which is the actual truth. But for my part, if I fail to produce you yourself as my sole witness to testify to the truth of my statements, I shall think that I've accomplished nothing of importance toward solving the matter under discussion; nor, I imagine, will you believe in your own accomplishment if you don't procure me as your sole witness and leave all these others out of account. There is, then, one kind of refutation, as you think and many others with you; but there is a different one, as I for my part believe. So let us compare them and see if there will be any difference; for it is perfectly true that the matters we are disputing are by no means trivial; rather, they are practically the very ones which to know is noblest and not to know is most disgraceful: the sum and substance of them is either to recognize or to fail to recognize who is happy and who is not.

472

First of all, for example, let us take the case we are now discussing: You believe it is possible for a happy man to do wrong and be unjust, if it is true that you consider Archelaus to be unjust, yet happy. Shall we be right in defining your position in this way?

Pol. Perfectly right.

Socr. And I say this is impossible. So it is one point of diversity between us. Very well. Can a wrongdoer be happy at all if he meets with punishment and retribution?

Pol. Not in the least; he would be very wretched indeed.

Socr. But if the wrongdoer is not punished, he will be happy according to your account?

Pol. Yes.

Socr. But in my opinion, at least, Polus, the wrongdoer and the unjust man are completely wretched, yet even more wretched if they are not punished and do not meet retribution for their crimes; and less wretched if they are punished and chastised by gods and men.

Pol. What you are attempting to maintain, Socrates, is quite absurd.

Socr. Yet I shall try, my friend, to make you also state the same things, for I think you are a friend of mine. So, as matters stand, there are these points of difference between us. See if I am right. I stated in our previous discussion that to commit injustice was worse than to suffer it.

Pol. You certainly did.

Socr. But you said that to suffer injustice was worse.

Pol. Yes.

Socr. And when I said that wrongdoers were wretched, I was refuted by you.

Pol. And so you were!

Socr. At least you think so, Polus.

Pol. And I'm right to think so.

Socr. Perhaps. And you, on the other hand, consider wrongdoers happy if they aren't punished.

Pol. Quite so.

Socr. While I hold that they are completely wretched, though those that are punished are less so. Would you like to refute this, too?

Pol. Why, Socrates, this is still harder to refute than the other point!

Socr. Not harder, Polus, but impossible. Truth, you see, can never be refuted.

Pol. How do you mean? If a man is caught red-handed in a criminal plot to make himself tyrant and is arrested and tortured and castrated and his eyes are burnt out; and, after he has suffered all manner of torments of the worst sort, is forced to watch his wife and children being tortured; and at last is crucified or tarred and burned alive, this fellow will be happier than if he were to escape and become a tyrant and ruler in his state and continue throughout life doing whatever he liked, envied and congratulated by both citizens and foreigners? Is it this that you say is impossible to refute?

Socr. Bosh, my dear Polus! You're trying to give me a scare, not a refutation. And just now you were citing witnesses. Nevertheless please refresh my memory for a bit: did you say "caught red-handed in a criminal plot to make himself tyrant?"

Pol. I did.

Socr. Then neither of them can ever be happier than the other, neither he who unjustly compassed the tyranny nor he who was punished. Of two wretched men, neither can be said to be happier. Yet the more wretched is surely the one who escaped and became tyrant.—What is this, Polus? Are you laughing? Here's a new kind of refutation: when a statement is made, all one has to do is laugh it down without argument.

Pol. Now don't you think, Socrates, that you are refuted already when you make statements to which no human being could assent? If you don't believe me, ask any one of the present company.

Socr. Polus, I am not one of your politicians; last year, in fact, I was a member of the Council and, as my tribe held the presidency, I had to put a matter to vote whereupon I raised quite a laugh for not knowing how to put the question. So please don't ask me, on this occasion too, to put the question to the

474

company. But, as I said just now, if you have no better disproofs than those you have adduced, give me my turn at the argument to try the sort of refutation I think should be employed. For I know how to produce one witness to the truth of my assertions, the man himself with whom I am holding the argument (the others, the mob, I can dispense with); and I do know how to put the vote to one man at a time, though I will not hold conversations with a crowd. Consider, then, whether you wish, in your turn, to submit to a possible refutation by answering my questions. And I, for my part, imagine that you and I and everyone else believe that to do wrong is worse than to be wronged and that not to be punished for wrongdoing is worse than to suffer punishment.

Pol. And I for my part maintain that neither I nor anyone else can hold such a belief. To begin with, would you yourself prefer to suffer wrong rather than do it?

Socr. And so would you and so would everyone else.

Pol. Far from it! On the contrary, not I nor you nor anyone else.

Socr. So you'll answer, will you?

Pol. Most certainly. I am, in fact, eager to know what on earth you're going to say.

Socr. Answer me, then, and you'll learn. I'll put my questions just as though we were beginning the discussion. Which, Polus, do you think is worse: to do or to suffer wrong?

Pol. To suffer it is what I think.

Socr. And what do you say to this? Which is uglier: to do or to suffer wrong? Answer me.

Pol. To do wrong.

Socr. Well, then it's worse since it's uglier.

Pol. Not at all, not at all!

Socr. I understand: it appears that you don't consider good and beautiful, or bad and ugly, the same thing.

Pol. I certainly don't.

Socr. But what of this? All beautiful things, such as bodies and colors, figures and sounds and pursuits—is it with reference to no standard at all that you term each one of them beautiful? In the first place, for instance, when you term beautiful bodies 'beautiful,' is it not either with reference to some utility, some use to which they may be put, that you do so, or with reference to some pleasure which produces delight from contemplation of the bodies? Can you adduce any other points of reference in discussing the beauty of a body?

Pol. No, I can't.

Socr. And is it the same with everything else, such as figures and colors? Do you term them beautiful because of some pleasure or utility, or for both these reasons?

Pol. I do.

Socr. And is it the very same way with sounds and everything that pertains to music?

Pol. Yes.

Socr. And further, in regard to laws and pursuits, their beauty is not, surely, to be found beyond these limits, but resides either in their utility or their beauty, or in both.

Pol. That is also my opinion.

Socr. And so again the beauty of learning is precisely the same?

Pol. Quite so; and now, at any rate, Socrates, you are defining admirably when you delimit the beautiful by pleasure and by what is good.

Socr. Then we may delimit the ugly by opposites, by pain and evil?

Pol. We shall have to.

Socr. When, therefore, one of two beautiful things is more beautiful than the other, it is more beautiful by surpassing the other in one or both of these qualities, in pleasure or utility, or in both.

Pol. Quite so.

Socr. And so likewise when, of two ugly things, one is uglier, it is uglier by surpassing the other in pain or evil. Is not this a necessary consequence?

Pol. Yes.

Socr. Come then, what were we saying just now about doing and suffering wrong? Weren't you saying that it is worse to suffer wrong, but that to do wrong was uglier?

Pol. I was.

475

Socr. Then if it is really true that to do wrong is uglier than to suffer it, it is either more painful and uglier by excess of pain, or uglier by excess of evil, or by both. Is not this also a necessary consequence?

Pol. How can it help being so?

Socr. In the first place, then, let us see whether doing wrong surpasses suffering it by excess of pain, and whether evil-doers feel more pain than those they wrong.

Pol. Surely not the latter, Socrates!

Socr. Well then, evil-doing does not exceed in painfulness.

Pol. Of course it doesn't.

Socr. Then if it doesn't exceed in pain, it can't, of course, exceed in both.

Pol. It doesn't seem so.

Socr. Then all that is left is the other.

Pol. Yes.

Socr. In evil, that is.

Pol. It looks that way.

Socr. So, then, it is by excess of evil that doing wrong must be worse than suffering it.

Pol. Obviously so.

Socr. Then is it not admitted by the vast majority, as it was by you in our discussion a little while ago, that to do wrong is uglier than to suffer it?

Pol. Yes.

Socr. And now, at least, it has turned out to be worse.

Pol. It looks that way.

Socr. Would you, then, prefer the worse and the uglier thing to that which is less so? Don't hesitate to answer, Polus; it will do you no harm. Submit yourself bravely to reason, as you would to a physician, and answer yes or no to my questions.

Pol. Well, Socrates, I would not prefer it.

Socr. Would anyone else?

Pol. I guess not, according to this argument, at least.

Socr. Then I was right in saying that neither you nor I nor anybody else in the world would prefer to do wrong rather than to suffer it. For, of the two, wrongdoing is worse.

Pol. It seems that way.

Socr. So you see, Polus, that when one method of proof is put beside the other, there is no comparison. Everyone in the world, except myself, agrees with you, whereas you and you alone are enough for me, both in assent and as a witness; your vote alone is enough for me to receive; I may dismiss the others. So much for this portion of our discussion. 476

Next, let us examine the second point on which we differed: whether for the wrongdoer to be punished is the greatest of evils, as you thought; or whether it is a greater one for him not to be punished, as was my opinion. Let us examine the question in this way: do you consider being brought to justice and being rightly punished for one's crimes the same thing?

Pol. I do.

Socr. Are you prepared to admit that all just acts are beautiful in proportion to their justice? Think carefully before you answer.

Pol. Yes, Socrates, I really do think so.

Socr. Then consider this point also: when a man performs any act, must there be something to be operated upon by the agent?

Pol. I believe so.

Socr. And does that something undergo what the agent performs, receiving an impression of the same sort as the agent's action? Here's an example of what I mean: if a man performs the act of striking, something must necessarily be hit.

Pol. Necessarily.

Socr. And if the striker hits hard or quickly, the object struck must be hit in the same manner?

Pol. Yes.

Socr. So the effect on the object struck is of the same sort as the action of the agent striking?

Pol. Quite so.

Socr. So again when a man does the act of burning, something must be burned.

Pol. Naturally.

Socr. And if he burns severely or painfully, what is burned must be burned in precisely the way the burning agent burns it.

Pol. Quite so.

Socr. So also when a man cuts, does the same argument apply? That is, there is something which is cut?

Pol. Yes.

Socr. And if the cutting is big or deep or painful, the cut made in the object which is being cut will be of the same sort as the cuts of the cutting agent?

Pol. It seems so.

Socr. To sum up, then, see if you admit universally the rule I have just stated: what the agent does is reproduced exactly in the object on which he operates.

Pol. Yes, I agree.

Socr. Well then, with these admissions made, let me ask you whether being brought to justice is to undergo something or to do it?

Pol. Necessarily, Socrates, it is to undergo.

Socr. Then it is at the hands of some agent or other?

Pol. Naturally; at the hands of the man who inflicts the punishment.

Socr. And does a man who punishes rightly punish justly?

Pol. Yes.

Socr. Is his action just or unjust?

Pol. It is just.

Socr. Then a man who is punished suffers justly in being brought to justice.

Pol. It seems so.

Socr. And what is just, I believe, we have admitted to be beautiful.

Pol. Quite so.

Socr. Then of this pair, one performs, the other suffers beautiful acts.

Pol. Yes.

477   *Socr.* Accordingly, if the acts are beautiful, they are good, being either pleasant or useful?

Pol. It must be so.

Socr. So a man who is brought to justice suffers what is good.

Pol. It looks like it.

Socr. Then he is benefited?

Pol. Yes.

Socr. And is it the kind of benefit that I mean? Namely, that his soul is improved if he is justly punished.

Pol. It is quite likely.

Socr. Then a man who is brought to justice is rid of the vice of his soul?

Pol. Yes.

Socr. And is not that to be rid of the greatest evil? Look at it this way. If you examine a man's pecuniary condition, do you see any evil other than poverty?

Pol. No, no evil but poverty.

Socr. What of physical condition? Would you say the evil there is weakness or disease or ugliness and the like?

Pol. Yes, I would.

Socr. And, in the same way, do you think there is any vice in the soul?

Pol. Naturally.

Socr. Wouldn't you call it injustice or ignorance or cowardice and the like?

Pol. Certainly.

Socr. So then in material possessions, in body, and in soul, these three, you have postulated three defects, poverty, disease, injustice?

Pol. Yes.

Socr. Which, then, of these defects is the ugliest? Isn't it injustice—in a word, depravity of soul?

Pol. Yes, by far.

Socr. So if it is ugliest, it is also worst?

Pol. How do you mean, Socrates?

Socr. Just this: It follows from our admissions in the preceding discussion that what produces either the greatest pain or harm, or both, is in every case ugliest.

Pol. Absolutely.

Socr. And have we now admitted that injustice or, generally speaking, evil in the soul is ugliest?

Pol. We have indeed.

Socr. Then is it ugliest as being most distressing, that is, surpassing in pain or in harm, or in both?

Pol. It must be.

Socr. Is, then, to be unjust and unprincipled and cowardly and ignorant more painful than to be poor and sick?

Pol. No, I don't think that follows, Socrates; at least, not from what we have been saying.

Socr. Prodigious, then, must be the amount of harm and astonishing the evil by which the soul's depravity exceeds the others so as to make it the ugliest of all, since this is not, according to your account, brought about by pain.

Pol. So it appears.

Socr. Yet further: that which exceeds in the highest degree of harmfulness must, I think, be the greatest of all existing evils.

Pol. Yes.

Socr. Injustice, then, and lack of principle and the rest of the soul's depravity are the greatest existing evils.

Pol. So it appears.

Socr. What is the art, then, which delivers us from poverty? Isn't it the art of money-making?

Pol. Yes.

Socr. And what is the art to free us from disease? Isn't it medicine?

478 *Pol.* Necessarily.

Socr. And the one to free us from depravity and injustice? If you don't have an answer ready when the question is put in such a form, look at it this way: where and to whom do we take men whose bodies are sick?

Pol. To physicians, Socrates.

Socr. And where do we take unprincipled wrongdoers?

Pol. Do you mean to the judges?

Socr. To pay the penalty, isn't it?

Pol. I agree.

Socr. Is it, then, by the application of some sort of justice that those who punish rightly inflict their punishment?

Pol. Quite obviously it is.

Socr. So money-making rids us of poverty, medicine of disease, justice of unprincipled wrongdoing.

Pol. So it seems.

Socr. Now which is the most beautiful of them?

Pol. Which do you mean?

Socr. Money-making, medicine, justice.

Pol. Justice, Socrates, is far superior.

Socr. So then again, if it is fairest, it will produce either the most pleasure or utility, or both?

Pol. Yes.

Socr. Is medical treatment pleasant, then, and are those who submit to it pleased?

Pol. I don't think so.

Socr. But it is quite useful. Is that true?

Pol. Yes.

Socr. Because the patient is rid of a great evil it is worthwhile to undergo pain and become healthy.

Pol. Quite so.

Socr. Which, then, is a happier condition for a man's body to be in: to be cured or never to be sick at all?

Pol. Obviously never to be sick.

Socr. Happiness, therefore, as it seems, is not to be rid of evil, but rather never to have had it at all.

Pol. This is true.

Socr. What then? Of two men who have an evil either in body or soul, which is the more wretched, the one who is cured and rid of his evil or the other who is not cured and still has it?

Pol. It seems to me the one who is not cured is more wretched.

Socr. And didn't we say that to be brought to justice is to get rid of the greatest evil, vice?

Pol. Yes, that is what we said.

Socr. For I take it that it is justice which brings us to our senses, makes us juster, and serves as the art to heal vice.

Pol. Yes.

Socr. Then he who does not have vice in his soul is happiest of all, since this has been proved to be the greatest of evils.

Pol. Quite obviously.

Socr. And second happiest, I suppose, is he who gets rid of it.

Pol. It looks that way.

Socr. And he, as we said, is the man who is rebuked and admonished and brought to justice.

Pol. Yes.

Socr. And worst of all is the life of a man who is possessed by vice and cannot get rid of it.

Pol. So it seems.

Socr. And is he not the man who, while committing the greatest crimes and practicing the worst sort of injustice, manages to elude correction and punishment and being brought to justice, as you say Archelaus has contrived to do, as well as other tyrants and orators and potentates?

Pol. It looks that way.

Socr. It is a fact, my very dear friend, that such men have contrived for themselves much the same plight as that of a man who is afflicted with diseases of the worst sort, yet manages not to be brought to justice by the physicians for his bodily shortcomings and so is never healed, since, like a child, he fears cautery and the knife as painful. Isn't this your opinion also?

Pol. It is.

Socr. Such a man is ignorant, it seems, of the very nature of health and soundness of limb. From our present conclusions, in fact, Polus, it seems likely that this is the sort of conduct that characterizes those who try to escape justice: they perceive its painful element, but are blind to its utility and ignorant of how much more wretched it is to associate with an unhealthy soul than with an unsound body—a soul, moreover, which is corrupt and unjust and impious. To this end they provide themselves with money and friends and learn to speak as persuasively as possible, straining every nerve to avoid being brought to justice and rid of the greatest of evils. Now, Polus, if our conclusions are sound, do you perceive what follows from this argument? Or would you like to recapitulate?

Pol. Yes, if you don't mind.

Socr. In the first place, are injustice and wrongdoing the greatest of evils?

479

Pol. So it seems.

Socr. And has it further been shown that to be brought to justice is to be rid of this evil?

Pol. It seems probable.

Socr. But not to be brought to justice ensures a continuance of the evil?

Pol. Yes.

Socr. Wrongdoing, then, is merely the second greatest of evils; to do wrong and not to be brought to justice is the first and greatest of all evils.

Pol. It looks that way.

Socr. Was not this, my friend, the point in dispute between us? You were congratulating Archelaus, the greatest of criminals, because he enjoyed complete immunity from justice; while, on the contrary, I thought that Archelaus or anyone else who hasn't been brought to justice for his crimes must necessarily be wretched far beyond all other men. I held that in every case the man who commits injustice is more wretched than one who suffers it, and that a man who is not brought to justice is more wretched than one who is. Wasn't this what I said?

Pol. Yes.

Socr. And has it been proved that what I said was true?

Pol. Apparently.

Socr. Good. Now if all this is really true, Polus, what great use is there in rhetoric? It must, in fact, follow from our present conclusions that a man has to keep a very strict watch on himself to avoid wrongdoing and its abundance of evil consequence. Is this true? 480

Pol. It is.

Socr. And if either he or anyone he cares about does commit a crime, he should voluntarily go where he will get the speediest justice. He must hurry to the judge, as though to a physician, proceeding with all haste so that the disease of injustice may not become chronic and make his soul ulcerous and incurable. How else shall we put the matter, Polus, since our former conclusions remain unchallenged? Is it possible for the one to be brought into harmony with the other in any way but this?

Pol. What else can we say, Socrates?

Socr. Consequently when a man defends his own wrongdoing, or that of parents or friends or children or his country, if it is in the wrong, rhetoric will be of no use to us, Polus. Indeed, one might suppose the very contrary, that it is a man's first duty to denounce himself, and, to a lesser degree, one's household or friends on any occasion when they have done wrong. Crime must not be concealed, but be brought to light so that the criminal may pay the penalty and grow well again. A man must force himself and his friends to grit the teeth without flinching and ignore the pain, bravely submitting to the physician's knife and cautery in the pursuit of the good and the beautiful. If what he has done is worthy of the lash, let him offer himself for the beating; if chains, for the fetters; if a fine, let him pay it; if exile, let him go; if death, let him die, being his own and his friends' first accuser and using his rhetoric for this object only, that all their crimes may be made manifest and they themselves be rid of the greatest of evils, injustice. Is it this we shall say, Polus, or is it not?

Pol. Well, Socrates, it seems quite absurd to me; yet it does, no doubt, agree with what you said before.

Socr. Then either our previous findings must be disproved or this is the inevitable result.

Pol. Yes, that is certainly true.

Socr. On the other hand, we may reverse the situation. Suppose it is necessary to do someone an injury, either to an enemy or to anyone at all: in the first place one must take good care that oneself is not wronged by the enemy (this must be sedulously avoided). Now when our enemy wrongs someone else, we must do everything in our power, both in word and deed, to prevent his being brought to justice or arraigned before the judge; but if he is, we must devise how he may escape paying the penalty. If he has stolen a large sum of money, we must see to it that he doesn't make restitution, but keeps it, squandering it on himself and his family, against the laws of God and man. Or again, if he has committed a crime worthy of the death penalty, see to it that he doesn't die; that, if possible, he shall never die,

481

but remain immortal in his villainy; or, failing this, that he sh
live as long as may be, continuing as he is. It is for projects c
this kind, Polus, that rhetoric seems to be useful, since I really
can't see any great utility in it for a man who doesn't intend to
do wrong, if indeed it has any use at all; at least in our preceding discussion none came to light.

Call. Tell me, Chaerephon, is Socrates serious about this or is
he only joking?

Chaer. He seems to me, Callicles, to be very serious indeed.
Still, there is nothing like asking him.

Call. Well, that's just what I intend to do. Tell me, Socrates,
are we to take you seriously at this point or are you only jesting?
For if you're serious and what you say is really true, won't
human life have to be turned completely upside down? Everything we do, it seems, is the exact opposite of what we ought
to do.

Socr. Callicles, if human beings did not have certain feelings
in common (though they may vary a bit from man to man), if
each of us had merely his own private sensations unshared by
the rest, it would not be easy to demonstrate to another what
one feels. I say this with reference to the fact that at the moment
you and I are both experiencing somewhat the same emotion
and each of us has two objects of his love: I Alcibiades, the
son of Clinias, and philosophy; you the Athenian Demos and
the son of Pyrilampes.[12] Now I have noticed that in each instance, whatever your favorite says, however his opinions may go,
for all your cleverness you are unable to contradict him, but
constantly shift back and forth at his whim. If you are making
a speech in the Assembly and the Athenian Demos disagrees,
you change and say what it desires; and in the presence of this
beautiful young son of Pyrilampes your experience is precisely
similar. You are unable to resist the plans or the assertions of
your favorite; and the result of this is that if anyone were to
express surprise at what you say on various occasions under the
influence of your loves, you would tell him, if you wanted to

[12] His name also was Demos; so Socrates' play on words is "with the Athenian
people" (as a politician) "and with the like-named son of Pyrilampes."

speak true, that unless your favorites can be prevented from speaking as they do, neither can you. Imagine, then, that you are hearing just the same kind of excuse from me. Don't be surprised at my remarks, but rather prevent my love, Philosophy, from making them. It is she, my dear friend, who continues to say what you are hearing from me now; she is, in fact, far less capricious than any other love. For my Alcibiades says now one thing, now another; but Philosophy speaks always the same and, though you are now surprised at her words, you were present at the whole discourse. So either refute her on the point I just made and prove that wrongdoing, together with impunity from punishment, is not the very worst of all evils; or, if you are going to leave this unrefuted, Callicles, by the Dog, god of the Egyptians, Callicles will not agree with you and will be at variance with you your whole life long. And yet, for my part, dear friend, I do believe that it would be better for me that my lyre or a chorus I directed should be out of tune and loud with discord, and that multitudes of men should disagree with me rather than that my single self should be out of harmony with myself and contradict me.

Call. Socrates, you seem to me to be going mad with eloquence, like a true politician! And now you are prattling this way because Polus has fallen victim to the very treatment which he accused Gorgias of having received at your hands. For he said, I believe, that when Gorgias was questioned by you as to whether, when anyone came to him desiring to learn rhetoric but without a knowledge of justice, Gorgias grew ashamed and said he would teach him, complying with conventional morality, because people might grow indignant if he said he wouldn't; and it was through this very admission that he was forced to contradict himself, which is exactly what you are so fond of. On this occasion Polus was laughing at you, and rightly, too, as I think: but now, in his turn, he has suffered this same fate. From my point of view, what I cannot approve of in Polus' performance is precisely this· he conceded to you that doing wrong is uglier than suffering it, and it was from this concession that he got completely tangled up in the argument and, being ashamed to say what he really thought, had his mouth gagged. Now, Socrates, you know you really do divert the argument into such cheap and vulgar paths, saying that you're pursuing the truth, but really getting us into what is beautiful, not by nature but by convention. Yet these two are for the most part opposed to each other, nature and convention; so that if a man is timid and doesn't have the courage to speak his mind, he must necessarily contradict himself. So this is the clever trick you have devised to cheat in your arguments: if a man makes his assertions according to convention, in your questions you slyly substitute 'according to nature,' and if he speaks according to nature, you reply according to convention. So in the present instance, when doing and suffering wrong were being examined, Polus spoke of what was uglier according to convention, but you followed it up as though it were a natural principle. By nature, in fact, everything that is worse is uglier, just as suffering wrong is; but to do wrong is uglier merely by convention. For to suffer wrong is not the part of a man at all, but that of a slave for whom it is better to be dead than alive, as it is for anyone who is unable to come either to his own assistance when he is wronged or mistreated or to that of anyone he cares about. I can quite imagine that the manufacturers of laws and conventions are the weak, the majority, in fact. It is for themselves and their own advantage that they make their laws and distribute their praises and their censures. It is to frighten men who are stronger than they and able to enforce superiority that they keep declaring, to prevent aggrandizement, that this is ugly and unjust, that injustice consists in seeking to get the better of one's neighbor. They are quite content, I suppose, to be on equal terms with others since they are themselves inferior.

This, then, is the reason why convention declares that it is unjust and ugly to seek to get the better of the majority. But my opinion is that nature herself reveals it to be only just and proper that the better man should lord it over his inferior: it will be the stronger over the weaker. Nature, further, makes it quite clear in a great many instances that this is the true state of affairs, not only in the other animals, but also in whole states and communities. This is, in fact, how justice is determined: the stronger shall rule and have the advantage over his inferior. By what principle of justice, then, did Xerxes invade Greece or his father Scythia? One could, of course, cite innumerable examples of the same sort of thing. To my mind men are acting in accordance with natural justice when they perform such acts, and, by heaven, it is in accordance with law, too, the law of nature—though, no doubt, it hardly coincides with the one we frame when we mold the natures of the best and strongest among us, raising them from infancy by the incantations of a charmed voice, as men do lion cubs; we enslave them by repeating again and again that equality is morality and only this is beautiful and just. Yet I fancy that if a man appears of capacity sufficient to shake off and break through and escape from all these conventions, he will trample under foot our ordinances and charms and spells, all this mass of unnatural legislation; our slave will stand forth revealed as our master and the light of natural justice will shine forth!

484

It seems to me that Pindar, too, illustrates my point of view in the ode in which he declares that

> Convention is the Lord of all
> Mortals and immortals;

and it, he continues,

> Justifies the utmost violence
> With sovereign hand. My witness is
> The deeds of Heracles, for without payment—

I am only quoting approximately, for I don't know the whole poem by heart. But he does say that Heracles didn't pay for the cattle nor did Geryon give them to him when he drove them off, as though it were by right of nature that the better and stronger should possess the herds and all the rest of the property of his inferiors, those weaker than himself.

Here, then, you have the truth of the matter. You will become convinced of it if you only let philosophy alone and pass on to more important considerations. Of course, Socrates, philosophy does have a certain charm if one engages with it in one's youth and in moderation; but if one dallies overlong, it's the ruin of a fellow. If a man, however well endowed, goes on philosophizing throughout his life, he will never come to taste the experiences which a man must have if he's going to be a gentleman and have the world look up to him. You know perfectly well that philosophers know nothing about state laws and regulations. They are equally ignorant of the conversational standards that we have to adopt in dealing with our fellow men at home and abroad. Why, they are inexperienced even in human pleasures and desires! In a word, they are totally innocent of all human character. So, when they come to take part in either a private or a public affair, they make themselves ridiculous—just as ridiculous, I dare say, as men of affairs may be when they get involved in your quibbles, your 'debates.' Euripides put his finger on it when he wrote:

> Each shines in that which can attract him most,
> The task on which he spends the livelong day,
> The work in which he can surpass himself . . .

whereas a man shuns and vilifies whatever he can't do well, but praises his other work out of regard for himself, with the notion that this is the way to praise himself. 485

But the best course, no doubt, is to be a participant in both. It's an excellent thing to grasp as much philosophy as one needs for an education, and it's no disgrace to play the philosopher while you're young; but if one grows up and becomes a man and still continues in the subject, why, the whole thing becomes ridiculous, Socrates. My own feeling toward its practitioners is very much the same as the way I feel toward men who lisp and prattle like a child. When I see a child, who ought to be talking that way, lisping and prattling, I'm pleased, it strikes me as a pleasant sign of good breeding and suitable to the child's age; and when I hear a little lad speaking distinctly, it seems to me disagreeable and offends my ears as a mark of servile origin. So, too, when I hear a grown man prattling and lisping, it seems ridiculous and unmanly; one would like to strike him hard! And this is exactly the feeling I have about students of philosophy. When I perceive philosophical activity in a young lad, I am pleased; it suits him, I think, and shows that he has good breeding. A boy who doesn't play with philosophy I regard as illiberal, a chap who will never raise himself to any fine or noble action. Whereas when I see an older man still at his philosophy and showing no sign of giving it up, that one seems to me, Socrates, to be asking for some hard knocks! For, as I said just now, such a man, even if he's well endowed by nature, must necessarily become unmanly by avoiding the center of the city and the assemblies where, as the Poet [13] says, 'men win distinction.' Such a fellow must spend the rest of his life skulking in corners, whispering with two or three little lads, never pronouncing any large, liberal, or meaningful utterance.

Now, Socrates, since I have only the most friendly feelings toward you, my experience seems to be that of Zethus toward Amphion in Euripides' play (which I just mentioned). It occurs to me, in fact, to say to you much the sort of thing he says to his brother: "You're neglecting, Socrates, the things you ought to care for; in a childish guise you're warping the noble soul that Nature gave you. Never will you be able to counsel aright or persuade other with plausibility. Never will you devise a gallant plan for the service of a friend." And yet, dear Socrates— don't be angry with me, for I'm speaking as your friend! Don't you think it's disgraceful for you to be in the state I think not only you are in, but all those who go faring deeper and deeper into the abysses of philosophy? For as the situation is now, if anyone were to arrest you or any of your kind and drag you off to prison, declaring that you'd broken the law though you hadn't done a thing, you know perfectly well that you wouldn't be able to help yourself. You'd stand there, reeling and gaping and not have a thing to say. If the fellow hales you into court, though his accusations are never so unproven and false, you'll die the death if he chooses to claim the death penalty. How can this be wisdom, Socrates, this art that takes a good man and makes him worse, unable to help himself or save himself from the gravest dangers, save neither himself nor anyone

486

13 The Poet is Homer (*Il.* ix 441).

else, this art that lets him be stripped by his enemies of all his possessions and suffers him to live in his own country with absolutely no legal status? Such a man, if I may use a vulgar phrase, is one you can slap in the face with impunity! Now, my dear friend, take my advice: stop your refutations, take up the Fine Art of Business, and cultivate something that will give you a reputation for good sense. Leave all these oversubtleties to some one else. Should one call them frivolities or just plain nonsense? They'll only land you in a house where you'll be the only visitor! You must emulate, not those whose very refutations are paltry, but men of substance and high repute and everything else that is good.

Socr. If my soul happened to be golden, Callicles, don't you think I should be overjoyed to find a stone to test the metal, the best stone possible, which, when I applied it, if it agreed that my soul had been well cared for, then I would know that I was in a satisfactory state and never needed another touchstone?

Call. What is the motive behind this question, Socrates?

Socr. I shall tell you. I think, now that I've met you, I've met just such a lucky stone.

Call. How so?

Socr. Because I am convinced that whenever you agree with me about any opinion my soul proposes, then it must be the whole truth. It is my belief that a man who is going to test a soul on the correctness (or the reverse) of its life must have three qualities: knowledge, good will, and candor. You have them all. I run into many people unable to test me because they are not wise, as you are; others have wisdom, but won't tell me the truth because they don't care for me, as you do; and your two guests here, Gorgias and Polus, are both wise men and friends of mine, but they are somewhat deficient in candor and more modest than they should be. This must be so; for both of them have gone to such an extreme of modesty as to venture to contradict themselves before a large audience, and this on matters of the gravest importance. But you have all these qualifications which the others do not possess. Your education is a

487

good one, as many an Athenian can testify, and you are well-disposed toward me. How may I prove this? I shall tell you. I am aware that there are four of you who have gone into partnership in the pursuit of wisdom: you, Callicles, Tisander of Aphidnae, Andron the son of Androtion, and Nausicydes of Cholarges. Once upon a time I overheard you deliberating about how far one should cultivate wisdom. I remember that some such opinion as this prevailed: philosophy ought not to be pursued to the point of pedantic minutiae. Rather than that, you exhorted each other to make certain you did not become overwise and be ruined before you knew it. Now when I hear you giving me the same advice you gave your most intimate friends, it is a satisfactory proof that you are really well disposed toward me. Finally, that you are frank of speech and not bashful, you yourself assert and the speech you made a little while ago confirms it. This, then, is clearly the present state of the question: if there is any point on which we both agree, we may regard it as sufficiently tested by both of us, and we shall never again have to submit it to further proof. You could not have conceded it either through a failure in wisdom or by excess of modesty; nor again through a wish to deceive me, for you are my friend, as you yourself declare. Any agreement of us both must in very fact bear the stamp of a final truth. And, Callicles, the investigation for which you rebuked me is the noblest of all possible inquiries: what a man's character ought to be, what he should study and up to what point, whether he is old or young. As for me, be sure of this: if there is any error in my own way of life, it is not an intentional one, but comes solely from my ignorance. Please, therefore, do not stop the lessons you have begun to give me, but show me clearly what it is that I ought to pursue, and how I may come to possess it; and if ever you catch me agreeing with you now on any subject, and later neglecting to act on it, then consider me a complete dunce and don't waste time teaching me any more lessons, for I won't be worth it. Now please begin at the beginning and tell me again what it is that you and Pindar declare natural justice to be. Is it that the stronger should plunder the property of the weaker, that the better should rule the worse, and that the superior man should have the advantage over the inferior? Does my memory fail me, or is this what you said justice was?

Call. This is what I said it was, and I say so now again.

Socr. Do you also say that 'better' and 'stronger' are one and the same? For, to tell the truth, I wasn't able on your first statement to grasp what you meant. Is it the more powerful whom you call 'stronger' and is it the feebler who must pay attention to the more powerful? This is what you seem to have been demonstrating by the statement that large states proceed against small ones in virtue of natural justice because they are stronger and more powerful. It appears to assume that 'stronger' and 'more powerful' and 'better' and 'stronger' are the same. Please define this precisely for me. Are 'stronger' and 'better' and 'more powerful' the same or are they different?

Call. I shall be glad to tell you precisely: they are the same.

Socr. Then are not the many naturally stronger than the one, inasmuch as they make the laws to regulate the individual, as you yourself said just now?

Call. Of course.

Socr. The ordinances of the many are therefore those of the stronger.

Call. Quite so.

Socr. And they are therefore those of the better? For the stronger are much the better in your account.

Call. Yes.

Socr. Then their ordinances are beautiful by nature since, to be sure, they are those of the stronger.

Call. I agree.

Socr. Is, then, the opinion of the multitude that, as you just stated, justice consists in sharing equally and that it is uglier to do wrong than to suffer it? Is this so or is it not? And see to it that you, in your turn, don't get involved in false modesty. Does the multitude, or does it not, believe that justice consists in having a share that is equal, and no more? That to do wrong is uglier than to suffer it? Please don't begrudge me your answer, Callicles, so that if you agree with me, I shall have confirmation from you, obviously a man well able to discern the truth.

489

Call. Well, yes. That is the multitude's opinion.

Socr. So, then, it is not solely by convention that to do wrong is uglier than to be wronged and that justice is sharing equally. It is thus by nature also. It looks, then, as though you were not correct in your former statements, nor right in criticizing me by affirming that convention and nature are opposed and that I knew it and so took an unfair advantage in argument by diverting to 'convention' what was meant by 'nature' and to 'nature' what was meant by 'convention.'

Call. Here's a fellow who'll never be done with trifling! Tell me, Socrates, aren't you ashamed to be playing with words at your age? If a chap makes a slip in a term, you pounce on it as though it were a treasure trove! Do you really think I meant anything by the 'stronger' except the 'better'? Didn't I inform you long ago that to me the better and the stronger are the same? Or do you seriously believe that if a pack of slaves and ne'er-do-wells, who have nothing 'strong' about them except perhaps their bodies, get together and make pronouncements, I mean that these are ordinances?

Socr. So, wisest of Callicles', that's what you say, is it?

Call. It certainly is.

Socr. Well, dear friend, I too have had for some little time now a suspicion that your definition of 'stronger' was something like this; so I now repeat my question in real anxiety to know precisely what you do mean. For of course you don't think that two are better than one, or that your slaves are better than you because their combined strength is stronger than you are. Please start again at the beginning and tell me what on earth you mean by 'better,' since it can't be 'more vigorous.' And please, my gifted friend, try to teach me my primer in a milder tone, so that I won't run away from your school.

Call. What a piece of sarcasm, Socrates!

Socr. No, Callicles; that I swear by Zethus, he whose name you took in vain just now to indulge in a good deal of sarcasm against me. But come and tell me who it is you mean by 'the better.'

Call. I mean the worthier.

Socr. But can't you see for yourself that it is you who are uttering words with no meaning? Please tell me whether you mean that the better and stronger are the more intelligent or whatever they may be.

Call. Aha! Yes, good heavens, it is just exactly this and that most emphatically!

Socr. By your account, then, one intelligent man is many times stronger than ten thousand fools: he should rule, and they be ruled, and the ruler should have the advantage over the ruled. This seems to me to be what you are implying—and I'm not playing with words—if it is true that one is stronger than ten thousand.

Call. Yes, that is just what I mean. This, in fact, I conceive to be justice according to nature: he who is better and more intelligent should rule and have the advantage over baser men.

Socr. Stop there a moment. What do you say to this? Suppose there are a great number of us in the same spot, as on the present occasion, and we have in the common stock ample provisions to eat and drink. Suppose further that we are men of all sorts, some strong, some weak, but that one of us is more intelligent than the rest about such matters, being a physician. Though he is in all probability stronger than some and weaker than others, will he not still be better and stronger to care for the provisions, since he is more intelligent than the rest of us?

Call. Quite so.

Socr. Then should he, because he is better, receive more of the provisions than the rest of us? Or ought he, in virtue of his authority, have control over everything, yet in the consumption of food and its use for his own person should he refrain from taking advantage of us on pain of punishment? Should he merely have more than some, but less than others? And if, Callicles, he happens to be the weakest of all, should he, the best of all, have the least? Is that the way of it, my friend?

Call. You keep talking about food and drink and doctors and all such nonsense! But that's not what I mean at all.

Socr. Well then, by 'better' do you mean the more intelligent? Say yes or no.

Call. I do.

490

Socr. But shouldn't the 'better' have more?

Call. But not necessarily of food and drink.

Socr. I see. You mean, perhaps, more clothes? Should the most skilful weaver have the biggest coat and go about dressed in the most and the finest garments?

Call. What's this about clothes?

Socr. Well, shoes then. The man who is best and most intelligent about shoes should have the advantage. The shoemaker should, no doubt, have the biggest shoes and walk about shod in the largest possible number.

Call. What's this about shoes? You do insist on talking nonsense!

Socr. Well, if that's not what you mean, perhaps this is it: a farmer who is intelligent and genteel about cultivating the soil should no doubt have a larger share of seed and use the greatest possible amount of it on his own property.

Call. Socrates, you always keep saying the same thing over and over again!

Socr. Not only that, Callicles, but on the same subjects, too.

491

Call. I swear you absolutely never stop talking about shoemakers and cleaners and cooks and doctors! As though our conversation were about them!

Socr. Well then, will you tell us what things there are in which the stronger and more intelligent have the right to a larger share? Since you won't accept my suggestions, won't you tell us yourself?

Call. But I have been telling you for ages. In the first place, the stronger men I'm talking about are not shoemakers or cooks, but those who use their brains for directing politics in the way it should go; they are, in fact, not merely intelligent, but also courageous and capable of converting their designs into fact; they are not the sort to shrink back through any feebleness of spirit.

Socr. Now, best of Callicles', don't you see how different our complaints about each other are? You declare that I am always repeating myself and you censure me for it. I, on the contrary, maintain that on the same subject you never say the same thing twice. First, you defined 'the better and stronger' as 'the more vigorous,' then as 'the more intelligent,' and now you come along with still another solution: 'the better and stronger' are to be described as 'more courageous.' Come, friend, tell us finally once and for all who you say are the 'better and stronger' and with reference to what.

Call. But I have already told you that they are the intelligent and courageous in politics. These are the men who should rule the state, and justice consists in this: they should have more than the rest, since the rulers should have more than the ruled.

Socr. How's that again? More than themselves, my friend? What's this about rulers and ruled?

Call. What do you mean?

Socr. That every man is his own ruler. Do you think it unimportant for a man to rule not himself, but only others?

Call. How do you mean, 'his own ruler'?

Socr. Nothing subtle, merely the general definition: temperate and self-controlled, having mastery over his own pleasures and desires.

Call. How simple-minded you are! You mean those fools, the 'temperate'!

Socr. What! Anyone can see what my meaning is.[14]

Call. Of course he can, Socrates! How can a man be happy if he's a slave to anything? No, my friend; what is beautiful and just by nature I shall now explain to you without reserve. A man who is going to live a full life must allow his desires to become as mighty as may be and never repress them. When his passions have come to full maturity, he must be able to serve them through his courage and intelligence and gratify every fleeting desire as it comes into his heart. This, I fancy, is impossible for the mob. That is why they censure the rest of us, because they are ashamed of themselves and want to conceal their own incapacity. And, of course, they maintain that licentiousness is disgraceful, as I said before, since they are trying to enslave men of a better nature. Because they can't accomplish the fulfillment of their own desires, they sing the praises of temperance and justice out of the depths of their own cowardice. But take men who have come of princely

492

[14] For once the text of this dialogue, which is generally good, becomes quite uncertain in the preceding speeches.

stock, men whose nature can attain some commanding position, a tyranny, absolute power; what could be lower and baser than temperance and justice for such men who, when they might enjoy the good things of life without hindrance, of their own accord drag in a master to subdue them: the law, the language, and the censure of the vulgar? How could such men fail to be wretched under the sway of your 'beauty of justice and temperance' when they can award nothing more to their friends than to their enemies? And that, too, when they are the rulers of the state! The truth, which you claim to pursue, Socrates, is really this: luxury, license, and liberty, when they have the upper hand, are really virtue, and happiness as well; everything else is a set of fine terms, man-made conventions, warped against nature, a pack of stuff and nonsense!

Socr. With what fine nobility, Callicles, your lack of reserve enables you to tackle the argument. The fact is that you are now putting into words what other men think, but don't care to state aloud. And so I beg you to keep right on so that we shall really discover how to live. Now tell me this: you say that we should not repress our desires if we're going to live the way we ought to; we should let them grow as great as possible and procure their satisfaction from any source we can; and that this, in fact, is virtue?

Call. That's what I say.

Socr. In that case it is wrong to say that those who want nothing are happy.

Call. Of course; otherwise stones and corpses would be happiest of all.

Socr. But life would be terrible as you put the matter, too. I shouldn't, you know, be at all surprised if Euripides were right to say

> Who knows if all this life of ours is death,
> And death is life?

493 And perhaps we are really dead. At any rate I once heard a wise man declare that we are, in fact, dead here and now: the body [15] is really our tomb, and the part of the soul in which the desires are located is such that it easily yields to persuasion and shifts back and forth. So a clever fellow, doubtless from Sicily or Italy,

[15] Here begins a series of puns which are too complicated for exact translation.

put this into a fable and, playing on the word because of its susceptible character, he gave it the name of 'wine-jar' and the foolish he called the uninitiated.

In the uninitiated that part of the soul where the desires are located, the unprincipled part, the very opposite of watertight, he compared to a leaky jar, because it could never be filled. So now he, in contradiction to you, Callicles, points out that of the inhabitants of Hades (he means, of course, the world invisible)— these, the uninitiated, will be the most wretched since they have to carry water to their leaky vessel in a similarly perforated sieve. Now by the sieve, as my informant expressly told me, he meant the soul and he compared the souls of the foolish to a sieve because it is leaky: by their lack of conviction and their forgetfulness they cannot retain anything. All this, to be sure, is rather strange stuff; yet it does point out what I want to demonstrate, if there is any way I can, in order to make you change your mind and choose a life that is ordered and content with what it has in place of one of insatiable self-indulgence. Well, now, am I succeeding at all in persuading you to come around to the view that the ordered life is happier than the unrestrained? Or could any amount of such fables have any effect in changing your mind?

Call. The very opposite would be more correct, Socrates.

Socr. Come now, let me give you another metaphor from the same crop as the former. See if you don't say that, in a fashion, it expresses the difference between the two lives, the self-controlled and the unrestrained. There are two men, both of whom have many jars; those of the first are sound and full, one of wine, another of honey, a third of milk, and many others have a multitude of various commodities, yet the source of supply is meager and hard to obtain and only procurable with a good deal of exertion. Now the first man, when he has filled his jars, troubles no more about procuring supplies, but, so far as they are concerned, rests content; but the other man, though his source of supply is difficult also, yet still possible, and his vessels are perforated and rotten, is forced to keep on trying to fill them both night and day on pain of suffering the utmost agony. If such, then, is the nature of these two lives, do you still assert that the self-indulgent is happier than the orderly one?

494

Am I, or am I not, succeeding in persuading you by such arguments that the orderly life is better than the unrestrained?

Call. No, you are not, Socrates. For the man who is full has no longer the slightest taste for pleasure; his life, as I said just now, is the life of a stone. Once he's sated, he no longer feels pleasure or pain. But in the other life is the true pleasure of living, with the greatest possible intake.

Socr. So then, if there's much intake, there must also be much outlet; there will have to be large perforations for the excess to flow away.

Call. Why, of course.

Socr. Now it's a pelican's life you are describing, not that of a corpse or a stone. But tell me: is the life of pleasure you mean more or less the sort in which one feels hunger and consequently eats?

Call. That's it.

Socr. And feels thirst and consequently drinks?

Call. Yes, that is what I mean; and one should have all the other desires and be able to fulfill them and enjoy them and so live in happiness.

Socr. Splendid, my dear fellow! Please go on just as you've begun and try not to feel the slightest shyness, which I too, it seems, must endeavor to avoid. Now first tell me whether a man who itches and scratches, and has abundant opportunity for scratching, can live his life happily by continually scratching.

Call. What a strange creature you are, Socrates, just a plain old pettifogger at heart!

Socr. Yes, Callicles, that is how I came to startle Polus and Gorgias and brought out their shyness; you, however, must not be startled or shy, for you are a courageous fellow. Just answer the question, please.

Call. Well, I'll admit that one can lead a pleasant life scratching.

Socr. And if pleasant, then happy also?

Call. Of course.

Socr. And is it only my head that I scratch—or shall I extend the range of my questions? Just consider, Callicles, what you are going to answer if I ask you one after another all the questions which logically follow, the climax of which would be the life of a catamite. Is not such a life dreadful and ugly and wretched? Or will you dare to assert that men of this sort are happy if only they have an abundant supply of what they want?

Call. Aren't you ashamed, Socrates, to take the argument in this direction?

Socr. Is it I who take this direction, my moral friend, or is it the man who declares with such abandon that all who have pleasure, no matter how, are happy; the man who refuses to distinguish between good and bad pleasures? But come now, tell me once more whether you assert that the pleasant and the good are the same thing or whether there is any pleasure which is not good.

495

Call. If I say they're different, I'll be contradicting myself; so I say they're the same.

Socr. Callicles, you are going back on our original agreement. It will be impossible to continue our search for truth together if you are going to make statements you don't really believe.

Call. That's what you do, too, Socrates.

Socr. If that's really what I do I'm quite wrong in doing it, and so are you. My dear fellow, please consider whether pleasure from any source whatever is not the good. But if it is so, then not only the many shameful consequences I have hinted at just now will obviously follow, but many others as well.

Call. That's what you think, Socrates.

Socr. So you really hold to this opinion?

Call. I do.

Socr. Then shall we take you to be serious and attack the question?

Call. By all means.

Socr. Well, if you do think so, please clear up one point. May I suppose that there is such a thing as knowledge?

Call. There is.

Socr. And didn't you say just now that, besides knowledge, there was something else you called courage?

Call. That also.

Socr. And you meant, didn't you, to speak of them as two things, since courage is different from knowledge?

Call. Quite.

Socr. What follows then? Do you call pleasure and knowledge different or the same?

Call. Different, of course, you universal genius.

Socr. Then courage, again, is distinct from pleasure?

Call. To be sure.

Socr. Now, now, this we must not forget: Callicles of Acharnae [16] has declared that pleasure and good are the same thing, but that knowledge and courage are different both from each other and from the good.

Call. And we can't get Socrates from Alopece to agree to it! Or does he agree?

Socr. He does not; nor do I believe Callicles will either, when he takes the true view of himself. Now tell me this: don't you think that good and evil fortune are opposite conditions?

Call. I do.

Socr. Then, since these are mutually opposed, the relation between them must be the same as that between sickness and health; for obviously a man is not going to be sick and well at the same time or be simultaneously free of both health and disease.

Call. How's that?

Socr. Take as an illustration any part of the body you like. I suppose a man may have a disease of the eyes called ophthalmia?

Call. Of course.

Socr. And while his eyes are sick they can't be well at the same time?

Call. No, they can't; not at all.

Socr. But suppose he gets rid of his ophthalmia; does he then get rid of his eyes' health and finish up by losing both simultaneously?

Call. Certainly not.

Socr. Such a result would, in fact, be astonishing and irrational, would it not?

[16] Demes, or country districts, of Attica. In Callicles' reply there is a further play on the name, 'Socrates from Foxton.'

Call. Extremely so.

Socr. Whereas, I imagine, a man gains and loses sickness and health alternately.

Call. I agree.

Socr. And is it the same with strength and weakness?

Call. Yes.

Socr. And speed and slowness?

Call. Quite.

Socr. And is it so with the other good things and happiness, and with their opposites, evil things and wretchedness; does one alternately gain and lose each one of them?

Call. Yes, certainly.

Socr. Consequently, if we hit upon anything that a man may lose and possess simultaneously, it is obvious that this cannot be what is either good or bad. Are we agreed on this point? Think it over carefully before you answer.

Call. But I do agree beyond any question whatever.

Socr. Then let us return to our former admissions. Did you say that hunger was pleasant or painful? By hunger, I mean the state itself.

Call. Painful; it is, however, pleasant to eat when one is hungry.

Socr. I understand. Yet hunger itself is painful, is it not?

Call. I agree.

Socr. And thirst also?

Call. Very.

Socr. Then must I go further with my questions or do you admit that every sort of want and desire is painful?

Call. I admit it without further questions.

Socr. Good. But you do admit, don't you, that drinking when one is thirsty is pleasant?

Call. I do.

Socr. And this phrase of yours 'when one is thirsty' implies pain?

Call. Yes.

Socr. But drinking is the satisfaction of a want and is a pleasure?

Call. Yes.

Socr. So you affirm that pleasure is felt in the act of drinking?

Call. Certainly.

Socr. 'When one is thirsty,' at least?

Call. I agree.

Socr. While one feels pain?

Call. Yes.

Socr. Then do you see the consequence of this? You are declaring that pleasure and pain are felt at the same time when you say that a man drinks when he is thirsty. Or does this not occur at the same time or place, whether in the soul or the body, as you prefer? I fancy there is here no difference. Is this so or is it not?

Call. It is.

Socr. Yet you state that it is impossible for a man to fare well and ill at the same time.

497

Call. Yes, and I say so again.

Socr. But you have admitted that it is possible to feel pleasure while in pain.

Call. It looks that way.

Socr. Then to feel pleasure is not to fare well, nor is to feel pain to fare badly. And the result of this is that what is pleasant is different from what is good.

Call. I have no notion what you're quibbling about, Socrates.

Socr. I rather think you do, Callicles; you're only pretending. But let us continue on our forward march, so that you may acquire some notion of what a clever fellow you are to take me to task. Isn't it true that in all of us both the thirst and the pleasure derived from drinking ceases simultaneously?

Call. I have no notion what you mean, I tell you.

Gorg. Don't say that, Callicles. Answer him for our sake, also, so we may properly come to the end of the argument.

Call. But Socrates is always like this, Gorgias. He keeps on asking piffling little questions until he's got you!

Gorg. What's that to you? Your reputation is not at stake. Just let Socrates refute you in any way he likes.

Call. Well then, go on asking your finicky little questions, since Gorgias wants it that way.

Socr. You are a lucky man, Callicles, to be initiated into the Greater Mysteries before the Lesser. I didn't think they allowed it. So let us begin again where we left off. Is it true that everyone ceases from his thirst and his pleasure at the same time?

Call. I agree.

Socr. And is it the same with hunger? Does one cease from all the other desires and pleasures simultaneously?

Call. That is true.

Socr. Then pains and pleasures cease together?

Call. Yes.

Socr. But on the other hand, as you once admitted, good and evil do not cease together. Do you still admit that now?

Call. I do. What of it?

Socr. The consequence, my friend, is that good is not the same as pleasure, or bad the same as pain. One pair of them ceases simultaneously, the other does not, for its members are different. How then could pleasure be the same as good, or pain as bad? If you like, look at it this way, though this, too, may fail to satisfy you. Yet consider: those that you call good, don't you call them good because of the presence of goodness in them, just as you call beautiful those in whom beauty is present?

Call. I do.

Socr. Well then, do you call fools and cowards good men? At any rate you didn't just now when you were talking about brave and wise men. Is it not these that you call good?

Call. Of course it is.

Socr. Well now, have you ever seen a foolish child pleased?

Call. I have.

Socr. And have you never seen a foolish man enjoying himself?

Call. I believe I have. But what of it?

Socr. Nothing; merely answer.

498

Call. Yes, I have.

Socr. Have you seen a sensible man in sorrow or pleasure?

Call. I have.

Socr. Which one receives the greater pleasure and pain, the sensible or the foolish?

Call. I don't believe there's very much difference.

Socr. Even that will do. In war-time have you ever observed a coward?

Call. How could I avoid it?

Socr. Well then, when the enemy withdrew, which did you think received greater pleasure, a coward or a brave man?

Call. Both had pleasure, about equally, I think.

Socr. Never mind the difference. The point is that cowards also feel pleasure.

Call. Yes, tremendously.

Socr. Fools also, it appears.

Call. Yes.

Socr. When the enemy is coming at you, do only cowards feel pain, or do brave men also?

Call. Both.

Socr. To the same degree?

Call. Cowards more, perhaps.

Socr. And at the moment of retreat, don't they feel more pleasure?

Call. Perhaps.

Socr. Then fools and wise men, cowards and brave men, all feel pleasure and pain to a similar degree according to your statement; but cowards feel them more than brave men?

Call. That is correct.

Socr. But are wise and brave men good, while cowards and fools are bad?

Call. Yes.

Socr. Then both good and bad feel pleasure and pain to a similar degree?

Call. They do.

Socr. Are good and bad men, then, good and bad to a similar degree? Or are the bad even more so than the good?

Call. I swear I haven't the faintest notion what you're talking about.

Socr. Don't you realize that you are maintaining that the good are good because of the presence of good in them, and the bad are bad in the same way; and good things are pleasant and bad things painful?

Call. Yes, I do.

Socr. Then when men feel pleasure, good is present—that is, pleasure, since they are pleased?

Call. Of course.

Socr. Then those who feel pleasure are good because of the presence of good?

Call. Yes.

Socr. And with those who feel pain, it is because evil is present, that is, pain?

Call. Yes, evil is there, all right.

Socr. So it is because of the presence of evil that you term bad men bad. Do you still maintain this position?

Call. I do.

Socr. So the good are those who feel pleasure, and the bad those who feel pain?

Call. Quite so.

Socr. And are they more so if they feel more, and less so if they feel less, and about the same if they feel the same?

Call. Yes.

Socr. And do you maintain, then, that wise men and fools, cowards and brave men, feel pleasure and pain in a similar way, and that cowards experience them even more than the others?

Call. I do.

Socr. Then reckon up with me the results of our points of agreement, for whatever is excellent material for conversation and inquiry is still excellent when used twice over and again. We maintain that the wise and brave man is good, do we not? 499

Call. Yes.

Socr. And the fool and coward bad?

Call. Quite so.

Socr. And, yet again, a man who feels pleasure is good?

Call. Yes.

Socr. And one who feels pain is bad?

Call. Necessarily.

Socr. But good and bad feel pain and pleasure equally, and perhaps the bad man feels them more?

Call. Yes.

Socr. Then the consequence will be that the bad man is equally bad and equally good with the good man—or even better! Aren't those and our former conclusions the result of maintaining that pleasure and good are the same? Aren't they a necessary result, Callicles?

Call. It's quite a time now, Socrates, that I've been listening to you while I spoke my agreeable answers, perfectly well aware that if for a joke anyone gives you an inch, you'll seize upon it with childish glee! As if you really believed that I or any one else in the world didn't realize that some pleasures are better and some worse!

Socr. Ah, ah, Callicles! What a rascal you are to treat me like a child! Sometimes you say one thing, then you say another, just to deceive me. Little did I think when I started out that you were going to mislead me on purpose; I thought you were my friend. But as things are, I see that I was mistaken. It looks as though I'd have to obey the old proverb and make the best of it and take whatever you're willing to offer me. Well, now it seems that you maintain that some pleasures are good, some bad. Right?

Call. Yes.

Socr. Are beneficial ones good, and harmful ones bad?

Call. Quite so.

Socr. Those are beneficial which do some good, and bad those which effect some evil?

Call. I agree.

Socr. Would these be the sort you mean, if we took, for example, the physical pleasures we just mentioned, those of eating and drinking: are the ones good which create health or strength or any other physical capacity, and bad those which have the opposite effect?

Call. Certainly.

Socr. So, in the same way, some pains are useful, and some are bad?

Call. Of course.

Socr. Then is it the useful pleasures and pains that we must choose and set in operation?

Call. Certainly.

Socr. Not the bad ones?

Call. Quite obviously not.

Socr. In fact, if you remember, Polus and I agreed that all our actions should be performed for the sake of good results. Is it also your opinion that the aim of absolutely all our actions is the good and that for its sake all other things are to be done, not the good for the sake of the rest? Will you add your vote to ours and make a third?

500

Call. I will.

Socr. Then what is pleasant is like everything else: it is performed for the sake of the good, not the good for pleasure's sake?

Call. Certainly.

Socr. Is it, then, in every man's power to choose from among pleasures those which are good and those which are bad, or is there in each case a need for professional knowledge?

Call. Professional knowledge is required.

Socr. Let us, then, recall my remarks to Polus and Gorgias. If you remember, I said that some activities were concerned solely with pleasure, procured this only, and paid no attention to what might be better or worse; and there were others which recognized good and evil. Among those concerned solely with pleasure I put cookery as a knack, not an art; and among those concerned with the good I set medicine as an art. And now by the love of friendship, Callicles, please don't think that you ought to play with me or that your answers should be at random or contrary to your true opinion; on the other hand, don't take what I say as a joke, either. You do see, surely, that our conversation is on the subject which should engage the most serious attention of anyone who has a particle of intelligence: in what way should one live one's life? Should it be the one to which you urge me as being the activity which best befits a man—speaking in public, practicing rhetoric, engaging in politics in the current fashion? Or should it be this present life of mine immersed in philosophy? And what is the difference between the two of them? Perhaps the best way to discover this is to begin with the distinction I attempted to make a little while ago: when we have made it and agreed upon the fact that these two lives are actually distinct, we must inquire what the difference is and which one of them we should choose to live. It is possible that you do not yet catch my meaning.

Call. I certainly don't.

Socr. I'll try to make it clearer. Since we have both agreed that there is such a thing as a good thing and a pleasant thing, and that the pleasant differs from the good, and that there is a practical way of attaining each of them, a search for the good and a search for pleasure, will you tell me first whether or not you still agree with this position? Do you?

Call. I do.

Socr. Then to proceed: in regard to what I was saying to our friends here, please reassure me that my remarks seemed to you to be accurate. I was maintaining, in effect, that cookery didn't appear to be an art, but a knack; yet medicine was an art. My meaning was that the medical art has made an inquiry into the nature of what it treats and the reasons for the treatment and can give an account of each of them. The other, however, directs absolutely all of its unprofessional efforts toward producing the pleasure which is its only end and aim; yet it has not studied the nature of pleasure nor its causes. It proceeds with complete irrationality, so to speak, and no hint of calculation; only by mere routine and a sort of knack does it preserve any memory of the usual results, by which, of course, it may procure its pleasures. This, then, you must first consider and see whether it has been adequately stated. Consider also whether there are certain other activities that involve the soul, some of them artistic, so that they take some thought for the soul's best interests; whereas others ignore this and are, as in the case of cookery, concerned solely with the soul's pleasure, making no study of how it comes about or which pleasures are better or worse, caring for nothing but the gratification they bring, be it worse, be it better. To me, Callicles, it appears that there are such activities which I maintain to be a flattery whether of body or soul or anything else, whenever they are employed to minister to pleasure without consideration of better or worse. Now tell me: do you share our views on these matters or do you disagree?

501

Call. Oh, all right, I agree—to help you finish up your argument and out of 'gratification' to Gorgias here.

Socr. And does this hold for one soul only and not for two or more?

Call. Oh no; it holds for two and for many more.

Socr. Then is it possible to 'gratify' a large crowd, all together at the same time, without taking into consideration what is best?

Call. Yes, I imagine so.

Socr. Can you tell me, then, what activities there are that indulge this practice? Or rather, if you please, when I ask you, if you think one of them belongs to this class, say so; if not say no. First, let us think of flute-playing. Does it not seem to you, Callicles, that it seeks our pleasure only and has no other object?

Call. Yes, I think so.

Socr. And is it so with all similar activities, such as playing the harp?

Call. Yes.

Socr. And the singing of tragic choruses and dithyrambic poetry? Does it seem to be of this sort to you? Do you imagine that Cinesias, son of Meles, cares at all whether his utterances will make the audience better? Or is he preoccupied merely with gratifying the crowd of spectators?

502

Call. The latter is obviously the case, Socrates, at least with Cinesias.

Socr. Well then, what about his father, Meles? When he played his harp, do you think he kept his gaze upon the highest good? And perhaps he didn't even aim at great pleasure, for his music used to annoy the audience. Now think: don't you believe that all harp-music and all dithyrambic poetry have been invented solely for pleasure's sake?

Call. I do.

Socr. And what about the effort of that stately marvel, tragic poetry? Is all her aim and concern merely to gratify the audience? Or does she also strive not to make any pronouncement which, though it may be pleasant and delightful, is also bad? Does she boldly sing out what is useful, though unpleasant, whether the audience likes it or not? Which attitude do you believe to be displayed by tragic poetry?

Call. Why, it seems quite obvious, Socrates, that the effort is rather toward pleasure and the gratification of the spectator.

Socr. Did we not assert just now, Callicles, that such an attitude was flattery?

Call. Quite.

Socr. Suppose we examine any sort of poetry: if one were to strip away the music and the rhythm and the meter, would there be anything left but bare prose?

Call. Nothing, of course.

Socr. Is this bare prose to be directed at great crowds of people?

Call. It is.

Socr. Then poetry is a kind of public address.

Call. So it seems.

Socr. It should, consequently, be a rhetorical kind of public address; for you do think, do you not, that poets make use of rhetoric in their plays?

Call. I do.

Socr. Then we have now hit upon a kind of rhetoric addressed to a crowd of people made up of men and women and children alike, of slaves as well as free men. We are not able to admire it very much because we maintain that it is a form of flattery.

Call. Quite.

Socr. Good. What, then, is the nature of the rhetoric addressed to the people of Athens and of the other cities of free men? Does it seem to you that orators always speak with an eye on what is best and aim at this: that their fellow citizens may receive the maximum improvement through their words? Or do they, like the poets, strive to gratify their fellows and, in seeking their own private interest, do they neglect the common good, dealing with public assemblies as though the constituents were children, trying only to gratify them, and caring not at all whether this procedure makes them better or makes them worse?

Call. This question you are asking is no longer a simple one. There are, in fact, some orators who say what they say with

503

deep concern for their fellow citizens; but there are also others such as you describe.

Socr. That's good enough. For if this matter is really two-fold, part of it will doubtless be a form of flattery and a shameless method of addressing the public; the other may well be beautiful, a genuine attempt to make the souls of one's fellows as excellent as may be, a striving always to say what is best, whatever the degree of pleasure or pain it may afford the audience. But a rhetoric such as this you have never encountered. Or, if you are able to mention such an orator, why have you not already told me his name?

Call. Well. . . . I swear I can't name a single one, at least among the orators of today.

Socr. Are you then able to mention any of the older statesmen through the influence of whose public career the Athenians became better than they were before? For my part, I haven't a notion who such a man might be.

Call. What! Have you never heard what a good man Themistocles was? And Cimon and Miltiades and our Pericles, who died only recently and you yourself heard him speak?

Socr. Yes, Callicles, if the definition you once gave of virtue is really true: to fulfill desires, both one's own and those of others. But if it is not true, if we must substitute what we were compelled to accept in the subsequent discussion, that we should fulfill only those desires which make a man better, not those which make him worse, and suppose this to be an art— I am unable to name such a man from the group you proposed.

Call. If you only looked hard enough, you could.

Socr. Then let us examine the question impartially to see if this is so. Consider: will a good man, whose speeches are for the maximum improvement of his fellows, say anything at random? Will he not always have some definite end in view? Just as all other craftsmen keep their eye on the task in hand and select and apply nothing at random, but only such things as may bring about the special form he is bent upon effecting. Consider, if you like, painters and architects and shipwrights and any other craftsman you please; each one of them disposes every element of his task in a fixed order and adjusts the parts in a suitable and harmonious scheme until the whole has been constituted as a regularized and well-ordered object. And so it is also, of course, with the rest of the craftsmen, including those we just mentioned, who occupy themselves with the human body, trainers and physicians; they too, I presume, direct their efforts toward regularizing and harmonizing the body. Shall we accept this view or shall we not?

Call. Good enough.

Socr. Then a house which has order and harmony is a good house, and one in disorder is bad?

Call. I agree.

Socr. And the same is true of a sailing vessel?

Call. Yes.

Socr. And may we further apply the principle to our own bodies?

Call. Quite.

Socr. Now what about the soul? If it is in disorder, can it be excellent? Or must it have some sort of order and harmony?

Call. We shall have to grant this, too, to agree with our former conclusions.

Socr. What name, then, may we apply to the results of order and harmony in the body?

Call. I suppose you mean health and strength.

Socr. I do. Next, what name do we give to the results of order and harmony in the soul? Please try to think of the word and tell me as you did before.

Call. Why don't you tell us yourself, Socrates?

Socr. Well, if you like that better, I shall. And if you think I'm right, say so; if not, refute me, please, and don't let it pass. I think that 'healthy' is the right word for order in the body; from it health and the other physical excellencies arise. Is this so or is it not?

Call. It is so.

Socr. And the word for harmony and order in the soul is 'lawful' and 'law,' by which men become law-abiding and orderly.

These qualities, then, are justice and self-control. Do you agree or do you not?

Call. Let it stand.

Socr. Then it is these qualities which the moral artist, the true orator, will have in view in applying to men's souls whatever speech he may use; to these he will apply absolutely every one of his actions. Whether he bestows a benefit or takes one away, he will always fix his mind upon this aim: the engendering of justice in the souls of his fellow citizens and the eradication of injustice, the planting of self-control and the uprooting of un-control, the entrance of virtue and the exit of vice. Do you agree or not?

Call. I agree.

Socr. One must, I think; for what would be the use in offering to a sick, wretched body abundant food, no matter how delicious, or wine or anything else, when, properly considered, these may sometimes do no more good than their very opposites, or rather do it even less good? Is this true?

Call. Let it stand.

Socr. There is no advantage, then, I take it, for a man with a wretched body to live at all; for his way of life also must be wretched. Isn't this true?

Call. Yes.

Socr. It is, in general, only when a man is healthy that the doctors let him fulfill his desires, such as eating as much as he wants when he is hungry, and drinking all he likes when thirsty; but if he is sick, they practically never allow him to satisfy his appetites. Do you also agree to this?

Call. I do.

Socr. And, my dear friend, will not the same hold true for the soul? As long as it is in a bad way, it will be witless and uncontrolled, unjust and impious, and we must keep it from its desires and allow it no action except what will improve it. Do you agree or do you not?

Call. I do.

Socr. Because this is presumably better for the soul itself?

Call. Quite.

505

Socr. Then to keep it from its desires is to punish it?

Call. Yes.

Socr. So punishment is better for the soul than the lack of control which you recently advocated?

Call. I haven't a notion what you're getting at, Socrates. Suppose you try your questions on someone else!

[*Socr.* Here's a man who can't endure benefaction. He can't stand what we're talking about: punishment.] [17]

Call. I don't give a damn for a single word you say! I only answered your questions to please Gorgias.

Socr. Well, well. What shall we do now? Break off the argument in the middle?

Call. You're the judge.

Socr. They say, you know, that it's contrary to good morals to break off even a story in the middle; it needs a head, so it won't have to go running around without one. Why not complete your answers, so our argument can get ahead?

Call. What a slave-driver you are, Socrates! If you'll take my advice, you'll let this argument alone, or else do your talking to someone else.

Socr. Yet who else is willing? Let's not have our conversation go by the board.

Call. Why can't you finish it yourself? Talk to yourself and give yourself answers!

Socr. So that the words of Epicharmus may be fulfilled:

Where two men spoke before

I alone am to be equal to the task, though single handed! But it looks very much as though that's just what I shall have to be. Yet, if this is what we must do, I think that all of us should vie with each other in the struggle to learn what is true in the matters under discussion, and what is false; for it is to the common good of everyone of us that this should be made clear. So, then, I shall continue the discussion as seems best to me; but if anyone of you thinks that any statement of mine is con-

506

---

[17] The bracketed speech is probably an interpolation; at the very least it gives an odd turn to the methods of Socrates.

trary to the truth, he should take issue with me and refute it. For it is by no means from any real knowledge that I make my statements: it is, rather, a search in common with the rest of you, so that if my opponent's objection has any force, I shall be the first to admit it. This, however, is merely stated on the supposition that you wish to complete the argument; if not, let's say goodbye and go home.

Gorg. As far as I'm concerned, Socrates, I think you should not go yet. You must complete your argument and this, I believe, is the opinion of all the others, too. Personally, I have a strong wish to hear you continue the remaining portion by yourself.

Socr. Well, Gorgias, I too should have been pleased to go on conversing with Callicles here until I had paid him back Amphion's speech in exchange for Zethus'.[18] But since you, Callicles, are unwilling to help me finish the argument, at any rate please listen and take issue with me whenever I seem to be going wrong. And if you will be kind enough to refute me, I'll not be annoyed with you, as you have been with me; on the contrary, you'll be nominated my greatest benefactor.

Call. Go on and finish it up by yourself, friend.

Socr. Then listen while I recapitulate the argument from the beginning:

Are pleasure and good the same?

—They are not the same; on this Callicles and I are agreed. Is pleasure to be pursued for the sake of the good, or good for the sake of pleasure?

—Pleasure for the sake of the good.

Is that pleasant which, by its presence, gives us pleasure; and that good which, by its presence, makes us good?

—Quite.

But further: are we good, both we ourselves and everything else that is good, by reason of some excellence present in us?

—To me, Callicles, this seems a necessary consequence.

And again: the excellence of each thing, whether of utensil or of body or (to extend the definition) of soul or of any living thing—this excellence surely cannot be best acquired

18 See p. 54 above.

by mere chance, but by correct arrangement and by an art which is peculiar to each class individually. Is this true?
—I heartily agree.
Then is the excellence of each thing produced by order and arrangement?
—I should say so.
Then a certain order present in each existent thing and peculiar to it renders it good?
—That is my opinion.
So then a soul which has its own order is better than one which has none?
—This must follow.
And a soul which possesses order is an 'ordered' soul?
—How could it fail to be?
507   And an 'ordered' soul has self-control?
—Quite necessarily.
Then the self-controlled soul is good. My dear Callicles, I have no desire to change any of these statements. But if you do, please tell me.
Call. Keep on talking, friend.
Socr. I go on, then, to state that if the self-controlled soul is good, that which has the opposite disposition is bad; and this, of course, is the soul devoid of sense and discipline.
—Quite so.
Further, the self-controlled man will do what is right in regard both to gods and to men; for surely he would have no control if he did not?
—This is a necessary consequence.
And in his conduct toward men, when he does what is fitting, he will be doing what is just; in his conduct toward the gods, he will be doing what is holy. So a man whose conduct is just and holy must be a just and holy man.
—True.
Then, too, he must be courageous as well; for it is not the act of a self-controlled man either to pursue or to avoid what one ought not, but, on the contrary, to avoid and pursue what one ought, both actions and men, both pleasures and pains; he

must stand his ground and resist when it is his duty. So that the self-controlled man, Callicles, as we have defined him, just and brave and holy, must of necessity be completely good; and that the good man must do well and fairly whatever he does; and that, since he does his work well, he must be happy and blessed by the gods; and that, on the contrary, the wicked evil-doer must be wretched. Such a man will be one whose make-up is precisely opposite to that of the self-controlled man; in a word, the profligate whom you praised.

My position, then, is this and these are the things which I hold to be true. And if they are true, it appears that a man who wants to be happy must both pursue and practice self-control, and also flee from profligacy, each one of us as fast as his legs can take him. We must strive so far as possible never to stand in need of punishment; but if we or any one of our associates, either an individual or a government, needs chastisement, then they and we must submit to justice and be punished, if we are going to be happy. To me, at least, this seems to be the end and aim which a man must keep in mind throughout his life. He must turn all his own efforts and those of his country to bring it about that justice and self-control shall effect a happy life. He must not allow his desires to run riot nor, by striving to fulfill the endless torment of satisfying them, live the life of a brigand. Such a man could not be on friendly terms with any other man, nor with God, for he would be incapable of sharing; and where there is no sharing, there can be no friendship. Wise men say, Callicles, that heaven and earth, gods and men, are held together by the principles of sharing, by friendship and order, by self-control and justice; that, my friend, is the reason they call the universe 'cosmos,' [19] and not disorder or licentiousness. Clever though you are, you seem not to have paid enough attention to these matters; it has, in fact, escaped you what a mighty power is exercised, both among men and gods, by geometrical equality.[20] And it is your neglect of geometry

508

[19] That is, 'order.'
[20] "That is, proportion, which assigns to every man what is his due in accordance with his deserts" (Cope).

which brings about your opinion that one should strive for a
share larger than that which other men possess.

Well, then, either we must refute the present argument and
prove that it is not the possession of justice and self-control
which makes men happy, and the domination of evil which makes
them wretched; or, if the argument is true, we must examine
the consequences. There will be, Callicles, all those consequences
that preceded your question as to whether I was in earnest when
I maintained that if a wrong is done, one will have to accuse
oneself or one's son or friend, and it is for this purpose that
we must use rhetoric; also the point that you thought Polus
conceded to me through shame is, after all, quite true: namely,
that to do injustice is worse than suffering it in proportion as
it is an uglier act; and, finally, the fact that one who is going
to be a true rhetorician must first be a just man himself and
conversant with the principles of justice, which again was a
point which Polus said that Gorgias had conceded through shame
of denying it.

On the basis of these facts, then, let us try to examine the
reproaches that you lodge against me and see whether or not
they hold good. You say that I am unable to help either myself
or any friend or intimate, not even to save them from the
gravest dangers; that like an outlaw who is everyone's target
I am at the mercy of anyone who wants to slap my face (to
use your own spirited phrase), or to steal my money, or to banish
me or, if it comes to the worst, to kill me. And to be in such
a situation, according to your argument, is the most disgraceful
fate of all. Yet what my account of it is, though it has often
been stated already, may well be presented again. I deny, Callicles, that to be struck in the face unjustly is the most disgraceful of fates, nor is the mere fact of having my body or my
purse slit. No! It is the act of striking and slitting me or my
possessions wrongfully that is worse and more disgraceful; it is
robbery and kidnapping and housebreaking and, in a word, doing
me or my possessions any wrong that is worse and more disgraceful to the doer than it is to me who suffers it. These points,
as I am stating them now, have already been set forth in our

previous discussion and there fastened down and chained (if
I may put it rather bluntly) by arguments of adamant and
steel—or so it would appear. If you or someone yet more
vigorous are not able to break through them, then it will be impossible for anyone to speak correctly on such a subject in any
way other than the way I am speaking now. Remember that
my position has always been the same: though I have no real
knowledge of the truth of these matters, yet just as on the present
occasion, I have never encountered anyone who was able to
maintain a different position in such a discussion and not come
off covered with ridicule. Accordingly, I must assume that matters
stand as stated; if they really do so and if injustice is the
greatest of evils to the malefactor and if it is a still greater evil
than this (if such were possible) for the wrongdoer not to be
brought to justice, what sort of help should a man be able to
bring to his aid which, if he fail to do so, will render him truly
ridiculous? It will be, of course, the one which may avert from
us the greatest harm. Yet surely this must be the sort of aid that
it is shameful not to be able to give to oneself and one's friends
and intimates; and second in importance to it comes the inability
o ward off evil of the next importance; and third, evil of the
third importance, and so on. In proportion to the magnitude
of each evil is the glory of being able to ward it off and the
shame of not being able to do so. Is this true, Callicles, or is
it otherwise?

Call. Not otherwise

Socr. So given two evils, the doing of injustice and the suffering
of it, we must state that to do injustice is a greater evil, and
to suffer it a lesser one. With what, then, shall a man provide
himself to secure this double advantage: insurance from doing
wrong and from suffering it? Is it power that he needs, or will-
power? What I mean is this: can a man escape from being
wronged merely by willing to escape it, or may he escape it
by acquiring power to prevent it?

Call. Well, this at least is obvious: by acquiring power.

Socr. And what about insurance from wrongdoing? Is it
sufficient if he merely wills to do no wrong? Will he then not

do it? Or, to prevent his going astray, must he have acquired a certain power and art? And if he does not learn them and practice them, he may do wrong? Will you be kind enough to answer at least this question, Callicles: is it your opinion that Polus and I were right in our earlier argument when we were forced to admit that no one does wrong of his own free will and that it is against his will that everyone who does wrong commits such an action?

Call. Let it stand as you have it, Socrates, so that you may finish the argument.

[*Socr.* For this end, accordingly, that we may escape doing wrong, we must acquire a certain power and art.

Call. Quite.] [21]

Socr. What, then, may be the art which renders us immune from suffering unjustly, or suffering to the least possible degree? See if you agree with me on its identity, which I take to be as follows: one must either be a ruler in one's own country, or even a tyrant, or at least a friend of the existing government.

Call. Now see, Socrates, how eager I am to praise you when you put things nicely! This definition of yours, it seems to me, has been stated very well indeed.

Socr. Well then, see if you think this too is well stated: it appears to me that the strongest bond between friends is, as the wise men of old say, "Like to like." Don't you agree?

Call. I do.

Socr. So, then, when a savage and ignorant tyrant is the governing power, any man in the state who is far better than the tyrant will, of course, be feared by him and could never wholeheartedly become a friend of his.

Call. That's right.

Socr. Nor could a man who was much worse; for the tyrant would despise him and would not be likely to take his friendship seriously.

Call. That, too, is correct.

Socr. There remains worth mentioning, then, only one possibility of friendship for such a man: a person of like character

[21] The bracketed speeches appear to be a later insertion or amplification.

who blames and praises the same things and at the same time
is willing to be ruled and remain subordinate to his ruler. This
man will have great power in that state and no one will wrong
him with impunity. Isn't this true?

Call. Yes.

Socr. If, then, a young man under such a government should
happen to reflect, "How can I acquire great power so that no
one will wrong me?"—this, it seems likely, will be his method:
from his youth he will accustom himself to share the same likes
and dislikes as his master and make himself over into as exact
a duplication of the tyrant as he may. Isn't that true?

Call. Yes.

Socr. So then the young man will bring it about, according to
our account, that he gets great power and that no one wrongs him.

Call. Quite so.

Socr. But what about doing no wrong himself? Will he have
gained immunity from that? Isn't this most unlikely, if he is
going to resemble the tyrant who is unjust, and with whom he
will have great power? The very opposite, I think, will occur:
he will acquire the means of doing all the wrong he can and
at the same time remain exempt from the penalty of his misdeeds. Right?

Call. So it seems.

Socr. So, then, the greatest of evils will befall him: his soul   511
will become vicious and deformed by the imitation of his master
and his master's power.

Call. I don't know how it is, Socrates, that you always manage
to twist the argument around until it's upside down! Surely
you know that the man who imitates a tyrant can kill, if he likes,
anyone who doesn't imitate his master. He can seize all his
property.

Socr. Yes, I know it, friend Callicles, if, at least, I haven't
grown deaf, for I've heard it many, many times already, from
you and from Polus and from practically everybody else in
town. But you may also hear from me that if he likes he can
kill his victim, all right; but it will be a ruffian killing a good
man.

Call. Well, isn't that the very thing that arouses indignation?

Socr. Not in a sensible man, as the argument will tell you. Do you really think that this is the object of our lives: to live as long as possible, to lavish all our care upon the cultivation of those arts which may save us from danger—just as you keep urging me to cultivate the rhetoric that may keep me safe in the law courts?

Call. Yes, and I swear it's good advice I'm giving you.

Socr. Well, well, friend. And do you also have a high opinion of the art of swimming?

Call. Of course I don't.

Socr. And yet it too saves men from death when they chance to be immersed in something that makes such an art necessary. But if you think this too trivial, I'll mention a more important art, that of navigation, which not only saves men's lives, but their very bodies and all their property from the gravest dangers—just like rhetoric. And, moreover, this art is orderly and modest and does not put on airs or strike attitudes as if it were performing some terrific feat; yet it performs the same feat as forensic eloquence and brings you here safely from Aegina for the price of two obols; and if it be from the Black Sea or Egypt or some far place, in return for this great service, for having saved a man and his children and property and wife and disembarked them at the harbor here, it charges a couple of drachmae. And the master of the ship, the possessor of the art and the performer of this feat, comes ashore and walks along the quay by his ship with an unassuming demeanor. He is reflecting, I imagine, upon the uncertainty of whether he has benefited any of his passengers by not letting them drown, whether he has not actually injured some of them, aware as he is that he has put them ashore no better in either body or soul than when they embarked. He reflects, therefore, that anyone who has escaped drowning, yet is afflicted in his body with grave and incurable ailments, continues to be wretched because he is not dead and has not been benefited at all by the navigator; and, similarly, anyone who has in his more valuable part, the soul, many incurable ailments, will receive no benefit from con-

tinued life, whether he be saved from the sea or the law courts
or anything else. He knows, this navigator, that it is not better
for a wicked man to live; for his life must of necessity be an
evil one.

Now this is why it is not customary for the navigator to
put on airs, even though he saves our lives—nor indeed, my
worthy friend, does the engineer preen himself, though from time
to time his capacity for saving lives is not a bit less than that
of the general or anyone else you please, to say nothing of
the navigator. Sometimes, indeed, the engineer is able to preserve
whole cities. Do you think that this is in the power of the legal
pleader? And yet, Callicles, if he wanted to talk as the rest
of you do and glorify his business, he could tunnel you under
with his arguments, exhorting you to the duty of becoming en-
gineers since nothing else is of any importance. Believe me,
he has plenty to say. You, however, despise both him and his
art and, as though it were a reproach, you call him a mere
"engineer." You would never consent to marry your daughter
to his son, or yourself marry his daughter. Yet after the praises
you bestow on your own pursuits, what right have you to despise
either the engineer or the others I just mentioned? You may say,
obviously, that you are the better man and better born. But
if 'better' does not mean what I say it means and if virtue
is merely this: to save oneself and one's property irrespective
of one's character, then your disparagement of the engineer
and the physician and of all the arts which have been devised
for the preservation of life becomes ridiculous. Yet consider, my
dear friend, whether what is noble and good may not be something rather different from the mere saving of human life;
whether existence, over however many years, is not something
which a human being, who is at the same time a rational man,
must disregard. He must not cling to life, but surrender such
considerations to God and have faith in the old wives' proverb
that "None can escape his Destiny." Thereafter he must reflect
upon how he may best employ his allotted span of years, whether,
for instance, he should adapt himself to the form of the government under which he happens to be living. That is, in the

513

present case, whether you should make yourself as similar as possible to the Athenian people since you intend to be congenial to it and acquire great power in the state. Consider closely, my dear friend, whether such a proceeding would really be beneficial to you and to me. We do not want to meet the fate they say overtakes Thessalian witches when they charm the moon down from the sky; and upon the choice of such power in the state our dearest interests may well be staked. If you believe that there is any man on earth who can teach you an art that will at once make you powerful in the state and at the same time unlike it in temper (whether for better or for worse), in my opinion, Callicles, you're quite wrong. It is not merely an imitator that you will be, it is your very nature that will conform to the mob if you are going to enter into a real bond of friendship with the Athenian people and, I swear, with the son of Pyrilampes [22] as well. Whoever, then, may render you most like them will also make you the politician and orator you desire to be. Everyone, of course, is pleased with speeches that accord with his own way of looking at things and annoyed with a foreign point of view. Or do you have any objection, my dear fellow? Shall we reply to this, Callicles?

Call. I don't know how it is that your words attract me, Socrates. Yet I feel as most people do: You can't quite convince me.

Socr. It is because the love of Demos dwells in your soul, Callicles, and resists me. Yet if we go back to these same questions again and again and examine them more thoroughly, perhaps you will be convinced. Just remember that we decided that there were two ways of cultivating anything, whether it was of the body or the soul: one procedure is to aim at its pleasure, the other at its best good. The latter uses no soothing methods, it combats them. Was not this the distinction we made before?

Call. Quite so.

Socr. So the one method, that of pleasure, is worthy of no honor and amounts to nothing but flattery. Right?

Call. Have it so if you like.

[22] See p. 49 above.

Socr. But the aim of the other is to make the object of one's care as good as possible, be it body, be it soul?

Call. Quite so.

Socr. So then, when we take under our care the state and its citizens, must we not try to make them as good as possible? For without this endeavor, as we discovered sometime ago, there will be no use in any other benefaction we may attempt to provide; but first, in the case of those who are going to receive great wealth or authority over others or any other power whatever, their hearts must be made honest and good. Shall this be our statement?

514

Call. All right, if it suits you.

Socr. Suppose then, Callicles, that we were going to engage in public affairs and were urging each other on to architectural feats, the building of important edifices, walls or docks or temples: ought we first to examine ourselves and discover if we do or do not understand the art of building and elicit, too, the identity of our teacher? Should we or should we not do this?

Call. Of course we should.

Socr. Then, in the second place, we should consider this point: whether we have ever had occasion to construct a private building for ourselves or for any of our friends, and whether this building was beautiful or ugly. And if, after consideration, we found that we had sound and famous teachers and that, in collaboration with them, we had built many beautiful buildings, and even after graduating from their tuition we had continued to erect numerous works on our own initiative—under these conditions we might sensibly proceed to public structures. On the other hand, if we were unable to point out our instructor, or if we could point out either no building at all or only a number of worthless edifices, then it would surely be folly to attempt public works or to urge each other on to their perpetration. Shall we or shall we not accept these conclusions?

Call. Of course we shall.

Socr. And is this not true of all other cases? Suppose you and I were seeking the office of state physician and were encouraging each other to apply, on the supposition that we were competent

for the job. We should, of course, look into each other's records:
"Tell me, now, how is Socrates' personal health? Has anyone,
slave or free man, ever been cured by him?" And I should
conduct the same inquiry about you. If we did discover that no
one, foreigner or citizen, man or woman, had ever been cured
by us, I swear to God, Callicles, would it not be really ridiculous
that any human being should come to such a pitch of folly as to
attempt public service as a physician or to encourage others to
such a task before there had been even any private practice, often
with indifferent results, yet with a number of successful cures
and a proper training in the art? It would be like the proverb:
try to learn pottery by starting on a wine-jar! Don't you think
such conduct would be folly?

Call. I do.

515   *Socr.* But as the case is now, my dearest friend, since you
yourself are just beginning to enter on public affairs, and are
encouraging me to do the same and censuring me for not doing
so, should we not first look into each other's records: "Tell me
now, has Callicles ever improved any of his fellow citizens?
Is there anyone, foreigner or citizen, slave or free, who was
previously bad, unjust or licentious or stupid, and has become
through Callicles' efforts a good and decent man?" Tell me,
Callicles, if anyone examined you so, what would you reply?
Who can you say has become better through association with
you? Can you hesitate to reply if you are really able to point
to any of your own handiwork done in private practice, before
you attempt public service?

Call. You are trying to pick a quarrel with me, Socrates.

Socr. Believe me, it is not from quarrelsomeness that I ask
this question, but because I really wish to know how you think
politics should be conducted among us. When you have entered
upon the business of the city, will your chief care be the maximum improvement of us, your fellow citizens? We have repeatedly acknowledged that this is the chief obligation of the
politician, have we not? Have we or have we not? Please answer.
Well, I shall answer for you: we have acknowledged it. Now if
this is what an upright man ought to provide for his own city,

cast your mind back to what you said a little while ago about
the prominent figures of the past and tell me whether you still
believe them to have been good citizens: Pericles and Cimon,
Miltiades and Themistocles.

Call. Yes, I do.

Socr. Then if they were good, it is obvious that everyone
of them tried to improve the citizens. Did he try or didn't he?

Call. He did.

Socr. So at the moment when Pericles began to make his
harangues before the people the Athenians were worse than on
the occasions when he delivered his final speeches?

Call. Perhaps.

Socr. My dear man, there is no 'perhaps' to it at all. This
is a necessary consequence of our admissions if, indeed, it is
true that he was a good citizen.

Call. All right. What then?

Socr. Nothing at all. Just tell me this, too: is it commonly
reported that the Athenians became better under Pericles' influence, or the exact opposite, that they were corrupted by him?
This is the way I hear it: Pericles made the Athenians idle and
cowardly and loquacious and greedy by instituting the system
of public fees.

Call. That's the sort of thing, Socrates, you hear from the boys
with the battered ears.[23]

Socr. But here is something else I do not have merely on hear-
say, but you know it as well as I do: at first Pericles had a splendid
reputation and the Athenians never involved him in any sentence
which carried disgrace, so long as they were 'worse'; but when
they had been made 'good and honest' by him, at the end of his life,
they found him guilty of embezzlement and all but sentenced him
to death, clearly under the impression that he was a scoundrel.

516

Call. All right. Does that make Pericles a bad man?

Socr. Yet if he were the keeper of asses or horses or cattle, he
would be thought a bad one if the animals, when he received them
into his care, did not kick or butt or bite him, but became wild

[23] Excessively given to boxing in imitation of Spartan discipline; hence un-
patriotic.

enough to do all these things before he was through with them. Doesn't any keeper of any sort of animal seem to you a bad one if he takes over comparatively tame animals and makes them wilder than when he got them? Do you think so or don't you?

Call. All right, all right, anything to please you.

Socr. Then please me further by answering this question: is man also an animal or is he not?

Call. Of course he is.

Socr. And did Pericles have men in his care?

Call. Yes.

Socr. Well then, as we just now agreed, should they not have become more just under his care, instead of less, if it is indeed true that he was a good politician?

Call. Quite so.

Socr. Then, further, the just are gentle, as Homer says.[24] Do you agree? Is it so?

Call. Yes.

Socr. And yet he left them wilder than he found them, and that too against himself, which he could hardly have desired.

Call. Do you want me to agree with you?

Socr. If I seem to you to be speaking the truth.

Call. Let it stand, then.

Socr. If, then, he made them wilder, did he make them also more unjust and worse?

Call. Let it stand.

Socr. From this argument, then, Pericles was not a good politician.

Call. You're the one who says he wasn't.

Socr. And you too, in view of your admissions. But now tell me about Cimon. Didn't the very men he tried to serve ostracize him so that they could have ten years' respite from hearing his voice? And didn't they behave in precisely the same way toward Themistocles and, in addition, punish him with exile? And Miltiades, the victor at Marathon, didn't they vote to throw him into the Public Pit and, if it hadn't been for the president of the Assembly, in he would have gone? And yet these persons, if they

[24] *Od.* VI. 121, perhaps, though our texts do not say quite this.

had been good men in the way that you say they were, would
never have suffered such a fate. At least it is certainly true that
good charioteers are not those who keep their footing in their
chariots at the beginning; then, when they have trained their
horses and have themselves become more proficient in the art of
driving, fall out. Such a state of affairs is impossible either in
charioteering or in any other occupation. Or don't you think so?

Call. Yes, I do.

Socr. Then what we said before, it seems, is correct: we are
unaware of the existence of a single good politician in our state.
You admitted that there was none now, but mentioned some former examples and selected these we have just reviewed. They,
however, have been shown to be on a par with present-day speci-
mens. So, even if they were orators, they did not make use of the
true art of rhetoric (otherwise they would not have been dis-
carded) or even of the sort that merely flatters.

517

Call. Yet surely, Socrates, not one of the present breed has
come within miles of accomplishing such feats as did any one at
all of the elder statesmen.

Socr. Nor am I, my dear friend, censuring them, at least as
servants of the state; they seem to me, in fact, to have been more
serviceable than the present generation, and more capable of giving the state what it wanted. But as for transforming its desires
instead of toadying to them, as for persuading and coercing fellow
citizens to the point of self-improvement, there is not, in a word, a
whit of difference between generations. Yet this and this alone is
the task of a truly good citizen. I freely acknowledge that the
former age was cleverer at providing ships and walls and docks
and the rest of it than are our contemporaries.

In our argument, therefore, you and I are doing something
quite ridiculous: during the entire extent of our conversation we
have been continuously circling round to the same point—and
each in complete ignorance of what the other was trying to say. I,
for instance, thought that on many an occasion you had grasped
and acknowledged the fact that our method of treating the prob-
lem was a double one, concerned as it is with both body and soul,
and that one of them was subservient to the other. It is by that

treatment that we are able to provide food if our bodies are hungry, drink if thirsty, clothes if cold, and bedding and shoes and anything else we may physically desire. (I purposely repeat the same examples to make it easier for you to grasp the point.) Now the provider of these things may do so either wholesale or retail or be a manufacturer of them himself, a baker or a cook, a weaver or a cobbler or a tanner; so that there is nothing surprising in the fact that he regards himself as mainly concerned with the care of the body and is so regarded by others—at least, that is, by any others who do not realize that there exists an art which transcends all these, the combination of medicine and gymnastic. This art it is which is really concerned with the body's care and to it rightfully belongs the governance of the other crafts and the utilization of their products, for it alone understands what food and drink is good or bad for the perfection of the body, while all the other crafts ignore this cardinal principle. This is the reason, then, that they are servile, subservient, and illiberal in the treatment of the body, while the art of medicine and gymnastic is by right their master.

Now sometimes you seemed to comprehend that the very same facts and principles hold good for the soul as well, and then you agreed with my statements as though you understood what they meant; but a little later you came along with the opinion that there have been good and honest citizens in our state. When I ventured to ask you who they may be—look at the politicians you brought up! Do you know what seems to me to have the closest resemblance to them? It's just as though I should question you about physical culture and asked what men have been, or are, good trainers of the body and you were to answer in all seriousness, "Thearion the baker, and Mithaecus who wrote the treatise on Sicilian cookery, and Sarambus the shopkeeper: these have been wonderful physical trainers, since the first makes marvelous bread, the second cooks well, and the third provides excellent wine." And perhaps you would be offended if I were to say to you, "Man alive, you have no comprehension of true physical culture! You're merely listing servile fellows who cater to the appetites and have no understanding of the fine points. They, it may be, fill

and fatten men's bodies and so win their praise, yet finally bring
about the destruction of the flesh they had to start with. Yet
people will be too ignorant to hold the fellows who indulge them
with banquets responsible for their maladies and their loss of
weight; but much later in life, when their former surfeit, indulged
without regard to health, comes home accompanied by disease, then
they will blame those who happen to be in the vicinity and venture to offer advice; they will revile these innocent bystanders and
will even do them harm if they are able; but their predecessors,
those really responsible for their misfortunes, they will praise to
the skies. And what you are now doing, Callicles, is something extremely similar: you praise men who wined and dined our fellow
citizens and crammed them full of what they desired. Men say
that they made our city great, not perceiving that it is swollen
and ulcerous because of its ancient counselors. With no regard for   519
self-control or justice they stuffed our state with harbors and
docks and walls and tribute-money and all such nonsense; so when
this presumed attack of illness finally comes, they will blame the
advisers who happen to be about at the time, while praising to
the skies Themistocles and Cimon and Pericles, though they were
the true authors of the trouble. On you too they may perhaps lay
their hands if you don't watch out, and on my friend Alcibiades.
This they may do when they are losing all their empire, both the
recent additions and the ancient possessions, though you are not
responsible for their troubles—yet perhaps partially responsible.

Be that as it may, there is one quite irrational thing that I perceive happening every time a discussion of the elder statesmen
comes up. When the state lays hands on its politicians as offenders,
one hears them complaining and crying out against their harsh
treatment; they have done, they say, many splendid services to
the state and yet are unjustly brought to destruction by it. This is
nothing but a pack of lies; no leader of the state, not one, could
be unjustly ruined by the very city he controls. And it is likely
that the case of the self-styled politician is the same as that of
those who call themselves sophists. Sophists, in fact, with all their
cleverness, commit this extraordinary blunder: they pretend to
teach virtue, yet time and time again they accuse their pupils of

misdeeds, either of defrauding them of wages or of showing no gratitude for the benefits they have received. Now what could be more illogical than such a case? The pupils have become good and just; all injustice has been purged by their master; they have a firm hold on justice; how should they do wrong through a quality which is no longer theirs? Don't you think this is a strange blunder, my friend?—Callicles, you have actually forced me into public speaking by your constant refusal to reply!

Call. So you're the one who couldn't talk if there was no one to answer you?

Socr. It looks as though I could. This time, at any rate, I've had to go to great lengths because you simply wouldn't answer. But now, dear friend, please tell me in the name of friendship, don't you think it is illogical for one who asserts that he has made another man good to blame him for being bad, though *ex hypothesi* he has been made and guaranteed good by the very man who blames him?

Call. Yes, I think so.

Socr. And do you hear such statements from those who profess to educate others in the path of virtue?

520 *Call.* I do; but why mention such worthless fellows?

Socr. And why do you, then, mention those who profess to be masters of the state and devoted to its maximum improvement, yet who turn around and accuse it, when occasion serves, of the vilest wickedness? Do you think there is much difference between these classes of men? A sophist and an orator are identical, dear man, or at any rate they closely approximate one another, as I tried to tell Polus. It is your ignorance which makes you admire the one art, rhetoric, and despise the other. [Yet the truth is that sophistic is finer than rhetoric to the same degree that legislation is superior to judicial procedure and gymnastic to medicine.] [25] For my own part, I should have thought that public speakers and sophists were the only ones who had no right to blame, for causing mischief to themselves, the very thing they teach—if, that is, they are not going to accuse themselves, in one and the same breath, of doing no good to those whom they claim to benefit! Isn't that true?

[25] The bracketed words are probably an interpolation.

Call. Quite.

Socr. And, it seems, they should also be the only ones who could afford to make their services available to the public without a fee—if only what they said were true. Where some other kind of service is concerned, for example, when one is taught by a trainer to run fast, the defrauding of a reward is perhaps more comprehensible, in that the service may be thought to be gratuitous or there was no stipulation that the fee should be paid at exactly the moment the speed was imparted; for it is not, one would think, through lack of swiftness that men do wrong, but through injustice. Is this the case?

Call. Yes.

Socr. Then whoever removes precisely this, injustice, need never again fear to be treated unjustly; and he is the only one for whom it is quite safe to impart this benefit without stipulation, if, that is, anyone can really make others good. Is it not so?

Call. I agree.

Socr. Then this, it seems, is the reason why there is nothing disgraceful about taking money for advice on other matters, such as architecture or any of the arts.

Call. Yes, so it seems.

Socr. Yet only about this matter, how one may become as good as possible and govern one's house or one's country in the best way, it has come to be considered disgraceful to decline to impart one's advice until one receives money for it. Isn't that the case?

Call. It is.

Socr. The obvious reason is that this is the only benefit capable of making its recipient eager to requite it, and it has this result: it is thought to be a valid proof that the benefit has actually been conferred if it is requited; if not, not. Isn't this how matters stand?

Call. It is.

Socr. Then to which sort of treatment of our city do you urge me? Please define it for me. Is it to combat the Athenians until they become as virtuous as possible, prescribing for them like a physician; or is it to be their servant and cater to their pleasure? Tell me the truth, Callicles. It is only fair that, since at the beginning you were quite candid with me, you should continue in the same vein. So now speak out frankly and freely.

Call. Well, then I say: be their servant!

Socr. So, frankest of friends, you urge me to flatter them.

Call. Call yourself the lowest of the low, Socrates, if it gives you any satisfaction. But if you won't do as I say—

Socr. Please don't repeat what you've already said a hundred times, that anyone who wants to can kill me, so that I don't have to say again, "It will be a ruffian killing a decent man!" Don't say that anyone can strip me of whatever goods I may possess, so that I won't have to repeat, "But if he takes them, he won't know how to use them; since he took them unjustly, he will use them unjustly; and if unjustly, disgracefully; and if disgracefully, then to his harm."

Call. How confident you seem to be, Socrates, that nothing like this could ever happen to you, that you dwell out of harm's way, that you could never be dragged into court, quite possibly by some utterly vicious and debased creature.

Socr. Then, Callicles, I must really be a fool if I believe that in this city of ours anyone at all is exempt from the risk of any possible form of calamity. Of this, however, I am perfectly certain: if I ever am dragged into court and exposed to any of these risks, it will be, as you say, some vicious fellow that brings me there (for no honest man could ever so deal with the innocent); and, indeed, it would not be surprising if I were put to death. Do you want me to tell you why I expect such an outcome?

Call. I certainly do.

Socr. In my opinion I am one of the few Athenians (not to say the only one) who has attempted the true art of politics, and the only one alive to put it into practice. For this reason, then, I never carry on my habitual discussions with a view to gratification, but with my eyes fixed on the highest good, not on that which is merely pleasant. Being unwilling to follow your advice as to the employment of rhetorical tricks, I shall have nothing to say in the court room. The same situation that I described to Polus will apply to me: I shall be like a physician tried before a jury of children on the accusation of a cook. Just consider what defense such a man could make if he were caught in the toils of such a circumstance! His accuser will say, "Children, the defendant here has committed many offenses against all of you. The youngest of you he continues to maim by amputation and cautery; he drives you to despair by his starving and stifling; he forces you to hunger and thirst, then the drink that he gives you is bitter. How unlike he is to me, who have always regaled you with choice dainties of a tempting variety!" What do you think the physician caught in such a predicament could say? If he admitted the truth and declared, "Yes, children, I did every one of these things—for your good health!" How much of an outcry do you think a jury like that would make? It would be loud, wouldn't it?

Call. Perhaps; one would naturally think so.

Socr. And the physician would be at a complete loss what reply to make?

Call. Quite.

Socr. Such, however, is the experience I expect to have if I'm ever brought into court. There will be no pleasures provided by me that I can tell them about, pleasures which they count as benefactions and services (yet I am far from feeling envy for either the purveyors or those for whom they are provided). And if anyone accuses me of corrupting the younger men by perplexing them with doubts, or says that I criticize their elders with bitter words both in private and public, I shall be able neither to tell the truth ("Yes, and it is right for me to say all this and in doing so I am serving your interests, gentlemen of the jury") nor to utter anything else at all; so that, in all probability, there is no telling what may happen.

Call. Then, Socrates, do you think a man in such a situation and yet unable to defend himself is safe in this city?

Socr. Yes, Callicles, if he has this one advantage which time and time again you have agreed to acknowledge: if he were his own defense through never having said or done anything unjust to man or God. This line of self-defense we have repeatedly acknowledged to be the best one. If, therefore, anyone were to convict me of inability to provide this sort of aid either for myself or for anyone else, I should be utterly ashamed, whether my convic-

522

tion took place before many or before only a few, or even man to man; and if it were this inability that brought me to my death, I should be very sorry indeed. If, on the other hand, it is merely through lack of the art of flattery that I meet my end, I am perfectly certain that you will see me face death with composure. Of death itself surely no one who is not an absolute fool or coward can be afraid; it is to do injustice that men fear. And if the soul arrives in Hades burdened with a load of iniquities, that is the worst and last of all evils. And now, if you are agreeable, I should like to tell you a story to show that this is true.

Call. Well, since you've got through all the rest, you may as well finish this, too.

Socr. Then listen, as they say, to a very fine tale, which you may consider a myth, but I regard as a true story; for I want you to take everything I shall say as strict truth.

When, as Homer says, Zeus and Poseidon and Pluto took over the rule of the universe from their father, they divided it among themselves. Now in the time of Cronus there was a law concerning mankind, which holds to this very day among the gods, that any man who had passed his life in a just and holy fashion should at his death proceed to the Islands of the Blessed and dwell there in complete happiness out of the reach of evil; while the doer of evil and impious deeds should be sent to a prisonhouse of retribution and judgment; and this they call Tartarus. Now in the time of Cronus and in the earlier portion of Zeus' reign the judges were living men who judged their fellows while they too were still alive, since the arraignment of a man was held on that day when he was about to die; and for this reason the judgment was conducted badly. So both Pluto and the overseers of the Islands of the Blessed came to Zeus and reported that improper persons were being sent to both places. Then Zeus said: "I shall put a stop to this proceeding. It is quite true that the judgments are now conducted badly, for the defendants are brought to trial clothed and judgment is passed while they are still alive. There are many," he said, "who have wicked souls, but are clad in beautiful bodies and pride of race and wealth and, when judgment comes, many witnesses advance to their aid, testifying to the justice of their

lives. The judges are overawed by these; furthermore, they themselves are clothed, with the veil of eyes and ears and indeed the
whole body interposed before their souls as they sit in judgment.
All this becomes an obstacle for them, both their own clothing and
that of those they judge. Now first," said he, "we must terminate
men's foreknowledge of death, which they now possess. I have
already given orders to Prometheus to put an end to it. Next, they
must all be judged in nakedness, for judgment must not be passed
till they are dead. The judge also must be naked and dead in order
that the judgment shall be just, his very soul contemplating the
naked soul of each man who has died without warning, bereft of
all his kin, and all his trappings left behind him upon earth. Accordingly, since I recognized this state of affairs even before the
rest of you, I have appointed my own sons to be judges, two of
them from Asia, Minos and Rhadamanthys, and one from Europe,
Aeacus. So these, when they are dead, shall give judgment in the
Meadow at the Crossroads from which the Two Roads lead, one
to the Islands of the Blessed, the other to Tartarus. And
Rhadamanthys shall judge those from Asia and Aeacus those from
Europe; but to Minos I shall give the prerogative of passing
sentence on appeal when the other two have any doubts. And so
the judgment as to a man's last journey shall be rendered with
the utmost justice."

524

This, Callicles, is what I have heard and I believe it to be true;
and from the narrative I draw some such inference as this: Death,
as I think, turns out to be merely a divorce of two things, the soul
and the body; and when they have been separated one from the
other, each of them still retains much the same condition as it had
while the man was alive. The body retains its natural contours with
the marks of its upbringing and its experiences quite manifest. For
example, if a man's body was quite large while he was alive, either
naturally, or as a result of diet, or both, when he dies his corpse
will be large; if he was fat, the corpse will be fat; and so on. If,
again, he used to wear his hair long, the corpse will have long hair.
Or if he used to be beaten and had the marks and scars of lashes
or blows or other wounds on his body while he was alive, these
may all be seen on the body when he is dead. Or if he had any

limbs broken or distorted during life, in death the same are plainly
visible. In a word, whatever characteristics a man's body presented in life, these remain visible in death, either all of them, or
most of them for some little time.

Now this same state of affairs appears to me to hold true for the
soul also, Callicles. When it has been stripped of the body, everything in it becomes visible, all its natural traits as well as those
acquired from every habit and each pursuit. When, therefore, the dead appear before the judge, those from Asia before
Rhadamanthys, he causes them to halt before him and examines
each soul with no knowledge of its identity; often indeed, he has
laid hold on the King of Persia or some other monarch or despot
and discerned nothing sound in the soul; for it is deeply scarred
by the whip and full of festering wounds brought on by perjury
525   and crime, the imprint on the soul of its every act. He sees all of
it twisted by lies and impostures, crooked because it has received
no nourishment from truth; he sees it compact of distortion and
hideousness by reason of the irresponsibility and licentiousness,
the insolence and intemperance of its acts. And when he has seen
such a soul, he sends it, in all dishonor, straight off to the prison
where it is destined to enter and undergo the sufferings that are its
due.

Everyone who is punished, and rightly punished, ought either to
be benefited and become better, or serve as an example to others
that they may behold these sufferings and through fear become
better. Those who are benefited by their punishment at the hands
of men and gods are they that have committed only curable sins;
none the less their improvement must come through the pangs of
suffering both here and in Hades. Only in this way can they be
rid of their wrongdoing. But those who have committed the extreme of injustice, and have thus become incurable, serve as an
example to others; they themselves benefit not at all, since they
are incurable, yet others may do so when they observe these
malefactors suffering in the greatest, the most painful, and the
most fearful torments because of their sins, strung up forever in
that prisonhouse of Hades, an example, a portent, and a warning
to the unjust as they arrive below.

And one of these I say Archelaus will be, if what Polus tells about him is true, and any other tyrant who resembles him. One may believe, in fact, that most of these dread examples are drawn from tyrants and kings, despots and politicians, for it is they who, through irresponsible power, commit the most fearful and incurable crimes. Homer also is a witness to this, for he has represented kings and despots, Tantalus, Sisyphus, Tityus, as the ones who suffer eternal punishment in Hades; but no one has represented Thersites and other wicked persons of private status as suffering great torments on the ground that they are incurable. [A private person has not the power for great sin, and in this he is more fortunate than those who have.] [26] It is, Callicles, from the ranks of the powerful that the supremely wicked are drawn. Yet there is nothing to prevent good men from being found in this class also; and they, when they occur, are entirely admirable, for it is both difficult and most praiseworthy, Callicles, to live a just life when one has great opportunities to do wrong. Few, therefore, have survived this test, yet here and elsewhere they have sprung up in the past and there will, I don't doubt, be further examples in the future, honorable men endowed with the virtue of administering justly whatever one places in their charge. One most praiseworthy example, famed throughout Greece, was Aristides the son of Lysimachus; on the other hand, my dear friend, most powerful men become evil.

And so, as I was saying, the mighty Rhadamanthys receives such a man, knowing nothing else about him, neither name nor lineage, but only that he is bad; and on perceiving this he packs him off to Tartarus, putting a mark upon him to indicate whether he seems curable or not; and the criminal proceeds to prison and suffers whatever is his due. On occasion the judge may perceive a soul that has lived in holiness and truth, the soul of some private person or another; but most often, Callicles, as I should say, it will be the soul of a philosopher who has kept to his own business and has not meddled with others' affairs during his lifetime. Whereupon the judge is struck with admiration and sends him on to the Islands of the Blessed. Aeacus' role is just the same, [each of

526

[26] The bracketed words are probably an interpolation.

them sits in judgment with a staff in his hand] [27] while Minos, as overseer, sits apart; he alone has a golden scepter, just as Homer's Odysseus says he saw him,

Holding a scepter of gold and judging among the dead.[28]

So, Callicles, I have been convinced by these accounts; it has become my concern how I may present to the judge my soul in its healthiest condition. I relinquish, therefore, the honors that most men pursue and shall endeavor, by cultivating the truth, to be as good as I may during my life and, when I come to die, in my dying. And insofar as I am able I urge all other men (and you in particular I summon, thus countering your former summons to me) to such a life and such a contest as this, which I affirm to be worth all the contests here on earth put together. And I retort to your reproaches that it is you who will be unable to help yourself when that trial and that judgment which I have just described comes upon you. You will have to appear before the judge, Aegina's son; when he lay hands upon you and drags you before him, it is you who will stand there with gaping mouth and reeling head no less than I here; and it will be you, perhaps, whom they will shamefully slap in the face and mistreat with every indignity.

' It is quite possible that all this may seem to you only a myth, an old wives' tale, and you will despise it; nor would your contempt be surprising if with all our searching we could find anything better or truer than this account. But as it is, you will observe that the three of you, the wisest of all the Greeks alive at this moment, you and Polus and Gorgias, are unable to demonstrate the necessity of living any other life than this, which clearly brings advantage after death as well. Yes, in all our long discussion the other arguments have been refuted and this alone stands immovable: doing wrong must be avoided more sedulously than suffering it. Above all else, a man must study, not how to seem good, but to be so, both in public and in private life. And if he grows bad in any way, he must be punished; for this is the good which is to be rated second after being just: to become so

527

[27] The bracketed words are probably an interpolation.
[28] *Od.* xi, 569.

through making amends by punishment. Flattery of every kind, whether of oneself or of others, whether of the few or of the many, is to be avoided; and so rhetoric, like every other practice, is always to be used to serve the ends of justice, and for that alone.

Then join with me and be my companion on the journey to the place where, as the argument shows, you will be happy both in life and in death. And let others, if they like, despise you for a fool and insult you; even, God help us, confidently endure from them that ignominious slap on the cheek. There will be nothing terrible in this experience if you are a truly honorable man in the pursuit of virtue. Then at length, when we have really practiced virtue together as we should, we may, if it seems appropriate, apply ourselves to politics or deliberate about whatever else may attract us; for then we shall be better fitted for such deliberation than we are now. It would be disgraceful for men in what appears to be our present condition to put on airs as though we amounted to something, we who never hold twice the same opinion about the same subjects, and that, too, though they are of the greatest importance. Such are the depths to which our lack of true education has brought us. For our guidance, then, let us make use of the argument which has now revealed itself, declaring that this is the best way to spend one's days: to live and die in the pursuit of justice and the other virtues. Let us follow it, then, and urge on everyone else to do the same and to abandon that way in which you put your confidence and your exhortations; for your way, Callicles, has no value whatever.